COUNSELING STUDENTS

COUNSELING STUDENTS

Lessons from Northfield...
Echoes from Fountain Valley

PRESTON K. MUNTER
GRAHAM B. BLAINE
STANLEY H. KING
JANE H. LEAVY
DOUGLAS H. POWELL
JANET SAND
Harvard University Health Services

PAUL A. WALTERS, JR.
Stanford University Health Services

AH *Auburn House Publishing Company*
Dover, Massachusetts

Library of Congress Cataloging in Publication Data

Counseling students.

   Includes index.
   1. Personnel service in education—United States—
Case studies.   2. Student counselors—Training of—
United States—Case studies.   I. Munter, Preston K.
LB1027.5.C654   1988   371.4   87-35130
ISBN 0-86569-172-X

Printed in the United States of America

Dedication

This book is dedicated to Howard Jones and Dana L. Farnsworth, both extraordinary educators and counselors, each with a special sensitivity to the needs of teachers as well as students. Their capacity to translate their idealism about education into practical ways of meeting those needs has left a legacy to teachers and students everywhere. And their artful persuasiveness in encouraging academic administrators to make institutional responses to such needs has made the work and relationships of teachers and students immeasurably more satisfying. Wherever these men have been, the quality of academic life in general has been enhanced. Ultimately, Dr. Farnsworth's and Dr. Jones' efforts led to the widespread acceptance of counseling programs and activities as a valid and necessary part of contemporary education. In the Northfield–Fountain Valley Counseling Institutes, those of us on the faculty have had an extraordinary professional and personal experience in implementing at least one of their many visions. We acknowledge our debt to them happily.

CONTENTS

PREFACE

After the Northfield Counseling Institutes had been well established, Howard Jones urged those of us on the faculty to write a book about it. We agreed that it would be a useful thing to do and talked about it on many occasions, but somehow never got to it. Two years ago, with the silver anniversary of the Institute clearly on the horizon, we finally decided to fulfill our commitment to Dr. Jones. In writing the book, our intent has been to set down some of the basic lessons we have learned at Fountain Valley as well as at Northfield. We have not tried to develop a new theory of counseling, or even to convert the experience of the Institute into a cohesive, stylistically uniform text on counseling. Nor have we tried to present a sample of what the Institute is like, being fully aware that the essence of that experience lies inescapably in being present at East Northfield or Colorado Springs, listening, doing, and, above all, *feeling* in ways that are just not possible to convey or describe precisely or fully in print. So we have chosen to write about what seem to us to be some of the central and basic lessons that have developed out of the Institute year by year. In doing so, we have tried diligently to preserve the individual styles of each member of the faculty. They are, after all, a central element of the Institute experience. What is virtually impossible to convey is the quality of the interactions among us as a faculty, and between us and the participants. Those interactions are undoubtedly what make each Institute as powerful an experience as it consistently seems to be. But our hope is that the book gives a reasonably accurate picture and sense of the Institute experience and even some of its "feel." If it does, then we will have achieved one of our goals in writing it. And if there appears to be a special point of view towards counseling, if not a theory, so much the better.

So, this book celebrates the twenty-fifth year of the Northfield Counseling Institute and the fifth of the Fountain Valley Institute. No one is more surprised than we that they have continued and prospered as long as they have and are still going strong—stronger than ever, in fact. We are proud of what we have accomplished in these twin enterprises. At the same time we are pleased beyond measure to celebrate their anniversaries in this fashion. We hope that these pages are proper and acceptable evidence that our pride and pleasure are justified.

THE AUTHORS

ACKNOWLEDGMENTS

The authors wish to express their gratitude and sense of obligation to all of the teachers, heads of school, coaches, nurses, school physicians, and administrators who have been participants in the Institutes at Northfield and Fountain Valley and at their own schools throughout the United States. We have been moved by their commitment to the tasks of counseling as well as to their teaching and to fulfilling the demands and expectations so universally placed on teachers. They have generously shared their rich experience with students with us, and we have tried faithfully to weave what we have learned from them into the structure and process of the Institutes. In major ways the success of our efforts is due to the continuing contributions of these extraordinary people.

We are indebted also to the administrations of each of the schools who have been host to the Institutes through these years. In particular, we wish to express our appreciation to Mr. Richard Unsworth, Headmaster of Northfield Mt. Hermon School, who has continued to give active, sensitive, and wise support to this venture and, in many personal and special ways, to the members of this faculty.

Similarly, we are deeply indebted to Mr. Timothy Knox and Mr. Eric Waples, successive headmasters of the Fountain Valley School. The courage and sense of excitement with which they provided their campus oasis as a second home for the Institute was infectious. We are proud that they have made the Institute the most favored activity of their summer program. We continue to be grateful that they were willing to assume the risk of undertaking the responsibility of sponsoring our workshop. Every summer we are reminded of our good fortune in having the hospitality of these unusually lovely campuses extended to us so generously and so openly. The peace and quiet of these beautiful settings play a key role in the success of this enterprise.

Through the years, a number of people at Northfield Mt. Hermon have administered the business affairs of the Institute there: Hilda

Beardsley, Norma Pelzel, Brenda Gibson, and Claudia Istel. To them we give thanks, with special acknowledgment to Irene Jerkowski who, for the past decade and longer, has administered the affairs of the Northfield Counseling Institute with scrupulous fairness to the applicants as well as with efficiency, good humor, and an acute business sense. We express our thanks also to Patter Field, who—like her colleague before her, Nancy Twinem—provides so responsively for the many individual problems and needs of the participants every June.

To Joan Michaud we address particular words of thanks. It was her vision, courage, and organizational skill both as administrator and manager which launched the Institute at Colorado Springs and saw it through the first five years. Her joyful spirit infuses a special quality that all of us treasure. In no less measure, we thank Virginia Stuart and Rebecca Jones, who have done their tasks of managing the Institute at Fountain Valley so effectively. We also toast the kitchen expertise of Gerald Squier and his team at Northfield Mt. Hermon and John Brown and his staff at Fountain Valley.

Finally, the authors wish to say thank you to John Harney and Eugene Bailey of Auburn House. Never has a book gone to press with so much intelligent care and professionalism and with such complete absence of discord as has been the case with this volume. The editorial pencil was wielded very actively but with a degree of skill, sophistication, and sensitivity to the feelings of the authors and respect for their style that has surprised and pleased us more than we can say.

THE AUTHORS

THE AUTHORS

GRAHAM B. BLAINE, M.D. is a consultant in psychiatry at Harvard University Health Services and a director of the Big Brother Association of Greater Boston. He has served as Chief of Psychiatry at Harvard University Health Services and as director of the Family Counseling Service of Cambridge. He is a fellow of the American Psychiatric Association.

STANLEY H. KING, Ph.D. is director of the Northfield-Fountain Valley Counseling Institute and a clinical psychologist. He was previously director of research and clinical psychologist and is currently consultant in psychology at Harvard University Health Services. He was also a founding faculty member of the Northfield-Fountain Valley Institutes.

JANE H. LEAVY, L.I.C.S.W., senior social worker at Harvard University Health Services, is a clinical social worker specializing in psychotherapy with individuals, couples, and children. An executive board member of the Massachusetts Academy of Psychiatric Social Work, she was a clinical therapist at the Harvard Law School Health Services and a co-founder of the Women's Counseling and Resource Center.

PRESTON K. MUNTER, M.D. is director of the Harvard Law School Health Services and a psychiatrist at Harvard University Health Services, where he has also served as Chief of Psychiatry. He is a diplomat of the American Board of Psychiatry and Neurology and a life fellow of the American Psychiatric Association.

DOUGLAS H. POWELL, Ed.D., a psychologist at Harvard University Health Services, is president of Powell Associates in Cambridge, Massachusetts, and is on the editorial board of the *Journal of Interactive and Eclectic Psychotherapy.* He was previously a clinical psychologist at the U.S. Air Force School of Aerospace Medicine and Chief of Psychology and Director of Training and Research at Harvard University Health Services.

JANET SAND, Ph.D. is a psychologist at Harvard University Health Services and has a private practice specializing in psychotherapy with individuals and couples. She was Chief Psychologist at Plymouth Area Mental Health Center and a counselor at Boston University Counseling Center.

PAUL A. WALTERS, Jr., M.D. is director of the Cowell Student Health Center, Stanford University, and associate professor of psychiatry and behavioral medicine at Stanford University Medical School. He was formerly the Chief of Mental Health Services at Harvard University Health Services.

BACKGROUND OF THE NORTHFIELD-FOUNTAIN VALLEY COUNSELING INSTITUTES

Preston K. Munter

The concept of the Northfield–Fountain Valley Counseling Institutes developed during the late 1950s and early 1960s. It was a logical extension of the advisory program at the Northfield School for Girls and the Mt. Hermon School for Boys, as they were then called. Dr. Preston Munter, succeeded by Dr. Stanley King, had been consultant to the schools for this program, specifically with reference to students' academic and personal problems. As a result of these consulting activities, the focus of the advisory program shifted from advising students in the traditional sense, to helping the faculty-adviser and the faculty as a whole to facilitate personal problem solving on the part of students themselves—that is, helping teachers to become counselors.

In the course of their work, Dr. King and Dr. Munter had had substantive discussions with Dr. Howard Jones, president of the schools, in response to his objective of helping teachers deal effectively with students' problems which might impede their academic progress or otherwise disrupt their growth and development. Out of these discussions emerged a plan to organize a summer workshop for training teachers to become counselors. In 1962–63, Dr. Jones and Dr. King pursued this idea and arrived at the notion of a joint enterprise sponsored by the Harvard University Health Services and the Northfield Schools. The idea was explored further at a subsequent meeting of Dr. Jones, Dr. Edmund S. Meany, headmaster of the Northfield School for Boys, Mr. Arthur Kiendl, headmaster of the Mt. Hermon School for Boys, Dr. Dana L. Farnsworth, director of the Harvard Health Services, and Henry K. Oliver, professor of Hygiene, and

xvii

Drs. King and Munter. It was agreed that both Institutions would sponsor such a workshop. Called the Northfield Counseling Institute, it was offered to private secondary school teachers in the summer of 1963. Dr. King was appointed director and Dr. Jones agreed to raise some seed money to minimize costs to participating schools. His efforts were successful, and the Howard and Bush fund of Hartford Connecticut contributed sufficient money to pay half the cost that first year and to set aside some funds to be held in reserve against the possibility of a second Institute another year. Dr. King agreed to recruit a faculty from the Harvard University Health Services staff and to work with them to develop a program for the workshop. In addition to Dr. Munter, Dr. Henry Babcock, then psychiatrist to the Harvard Business School, Dr. Graham Blaine, then chief of the psychiatric services, and Dr. Douglas Powell, psychologist, all agreed to participate.

The response to the announcement of the Institute was very positive. Interested schools were asked to enroll two teachers each on the premise that at least two would be required on site to develop a counseling program. Twenty-four schools agreed to participate. The first Institute consisted of 48 attendees, mostly teachers but a few coaches, school nurses, and heads of school. The Institute was conducted over a two-week period with the intervening weekend free.

The remarkable success of that first Institute encouraged everyone to attempt a second one in the summer of 1964, again partially supported by the funds Dr. Jones had raised. The number of participants increased to just short of 60, and again the Institute was very successful. On the basis of those two years' experience, it was decided to proceed without outside financial support in an effort to determine whether the Institute should and could stand on its own. The schedule was condensed to a little more than a week and, again, the response to the announcement was gratifying. Sixty teachers attended the third Institute at their schools' expense. From that third summer, every Institute has been completely subscribed, even after the number of participants was expanded to 72. Indeed, each year there is a scramble to get applications in on time by schools who are especially eager to enroll their teachers. Over the years, a waiting list has developed and persisted, despite many attempts to accommodate all.

There have been many changes in the Institute over the course of the past 25 years. Each year the program is reviewed and changed to take into account the invited comments of participants of the previous year, as well as the faculty's own observations and sense of the current issues in the world of teachers and students. The faculty itself has changed considerably: Dr. Babcock resigned after the second year and Dr. Walters, who had been a guest speaker the first two years, became a full-time member of the faculty. Jane Leavy also became a full-time member in 1975, increasing the faculty to six members and allowing the Institute to expand to 72 participants. In 1981, Jane Leavy took a sabbatical and Dr. Janet Sand, psychologist to the University Health Service, took her place. This not only increased the faculty to seven but brought the number of participants to 77. The size of the small groups, as well as the overall size of the group, became somewhat unwieldy at this point. As it happened, however, Dr. Blaine decided to retire from the faculty then, and the number of participants reverted to 72, where it has remained happily.

The next change—in some ways the most significant one—occurred in 1983 when the Fountain Valley Counseling Institute was established. Concurrent with the gradual increase in the waiting list at Northfield, Mr. Timothy Knox and Ms. Joan Michaud at Fountain Valley began investigating the possibility of establishing an Institute at their school. At first they explored the possibility of doing so as a joint enterprise with a school in California, but ultimately Fountain Valley decided to go it alone in a cooperative effort with Northfield. This course appeared to be advantageous in a number of respects, particularly in regard to reducing or eliminating the waiting list. Remarkably enough, the first Fountain Valley Counseling Institute attracted 48 participants and the second almost 60, as had been the case in the first two years at Northfield. Thereafter, it has had a full complement of 72. And in repetition of the pattern as it had developed at Northfield, Fountain Valley now has its own waiting list.

There have been some recent changes in the faculty. Dr. Douglas Powell, a founding faculty member, resigned from the Northfield Institute in 1987 to pursue heavily increasing research responsibilities. In addition, as this is being written, the last changes in the faculty have taken place. Two new members have been appointed: Ellen Porter-Honnet, Assistant Dean of Harvard College for Co-Education, and Dr. Mack I. Davis, Assistant to the Dean of the Harvard Faculty of Arts and Sciences, formerly the acting Director of the Harvard Bureau of Study Counsel.

The program, faculty, and cost for any given year are exactly the same for both Institutes. The announcements are sent out simultaneously and the choice of participants is based only on timing—June for Northfield, August for Fountain Valley—convenience, or personal preference.

The Institutes have had a significant impact on private secondary school education. They have had a major impact in some schools, especially in the East but also throughout the country generally and, to a limited extent, abroad. Measured in terms of the number of teacher contacts in both major Institutes and at the so-called "mini-Institutes" at individual schools (which regularly have numbered in the neighborhood of six to eight each year), approximately 20,000 private secondary teachers have had direct exposure to the philosophy, attitudes, and varied experience of the faculty of these workshops. An immeasurable number of teachers have, of course, had indirect contact through those who attended. During these years the notion of advising has been differentiated from that of counseling, and the legitimacy of that differentiation has been clearly established for classroom teachers, coaches, and administrators. Counseling students by means which the Institute espouses has taken a lasting, humanizing and, we believe, productive hold on this influential segment of the country's educational system.

Chapter 1

DEFINITION AND PHILOSOPHY OF COUNSELING

Jane H. Leavy

Teachers who attend the Northfield-Fountain Valley Counseling Institutes often bring a variety of predetermined ideas about the nature of counseling. They also come with diverse feelings about the subject that range from very positive to doubtful, or even to downright skeptical. Because of the range of attitudes and the variety of experiences with counseling among the participants, we have found it important to provide each group of institute participants with a conceptual framework for counseling—one which is basic and familiar to anyone who has worked in the field but also adaptable to the kinds of counseling situations which usually confront teachers.

What follows, then, is a working definition of counseling in pure form, not exactly as it may eventually be practiced by teachers, but containing the essential elements which we feel transcend the particular situation and apply in most school situations where counseling is being practiced. The definition also suggests a philosophy which links the work of counseling with the work of education. The kind of counseling we are teaching involves learning about oneself and being willing to take more responsibility for oneself and one's feelings, relationships, and behavior. The goal of each institute is to explore with the participants the ways this definition and philosophy can expand their role as teachers and enhance their work with students.

In the Institutes we define counseling as *a process by which one*

person (the counselor) attempts to understand and helps to clarify,
through listening with objectivity and empathy, those feelings in the
other person (in this case, the student) which impede growth, ma-
turation, and well-being. The objective implicit in this process is
self-discovery, which, in turn, leads to growth and increased self-
esteem in the student. There is a certain amount of mental health
jargon in this definition. Terms such as "process," "empathy," and
"self-esteem" appear everywhere in the mental health field, and to
some extent we feel it important to clarify what they mean to us and
to develop at the beginning of the Institutes a common framework of
meaning for them. In an effort to get away from jargon and build a
working vocabulary, we therefore need to explain how we define
some of these terms.

Counseling as a Process

First and central to an understanding of counseling is the idea that it
is a process, not a discrete event. It is in the nature of our work that
it needs to be carried out over time. In the first place, the relationship, the understanding, and the trust that need to develop between
the counselor and the student may not exist at the outset, and they
usually take time to develop. Second, the kinds of problems in students' lives that require counseling have sometimes taken years to
develop, and they also take time—though by no means necessarily
years—to be resolved. So it is well to recognize at the start that a
commitment to a counseling relationship with a student implies a
commitment to work over time.

The term "process" itself implies ongoing action and continuing
change, and it is meant in that sense on a number of levels. The counseling process is a dialogue, an ongoing conversation, a developing relationship, and—hopefully—a journey toward personal growth.
When we use the term "process," we therefore also mean to suggest
movement, growth, and change, as opposed to a static or one-dimen-
sional event.

What is the nature of the understanding of students which counselors attempt to achive in counseling? Every teacher has worked to
understand something difficult—for example, complex mathematical
concepts, historical events, or works of literature. The training of an
educator is based on the experience of learning and mastering a cer-

tain field and on a respect for what learning really involves. Genuine understanding or mastery requires a certain willingness to undergo a kind of immersion in the subject: to start from the simplest, clearest point and work over time to gather, pull together, integrate, and make a personal sense of things that explains matters which otherwise seem to be inexplicable.

So it is in counseling. The process by which counselors strive to understand is similar, although it does not follow the same logical patterns of other intellectual efforts. Usually people's feelings are not entirely rational, logical, or precise. More often they are irrational, ambiguous, and sometimes contradictory or paradoxical. The understanding of feelings requires a degree of submersion in the student's inner experiences that permits the counselor to make emotional sense of those experiences. It is toward an understanding of the emotional logic of the student that the counselor works, trying always to learn how that emotional logic organizes the student's experience of his or her life.

A Paradoxical Requirement: Objectivity and Empathy

Objectivity and empathy are two sides of one coin in counseling. These terms describe the basic stance of the counselor. Together, they describe an important tension in that stance. On the one hand, the counselor stands outside the experience of the student, retaining a certain distance, neutrality, or independence from what the student is feeling. But, on the other hand, the counselor seeks a kind of immersion in what she or he is hearing and works to achieve a strong *personal* sense of what the student is feeling. "Listening with objectivity and empathy," then, is no small feat. It requires balancing oneself between closeness and separation, listening from within the feelings and looking at them from without. This tension is difficult for any counselor to achieve. Inexperienced counselors have a special, though common, difficulty. They usually start out doing too much of one side or the other, either being too judgmental or overly identifying with the student's feelings. The art of counseling lies in learning to sustain and work within the tension of this dual stance by listening to, but not taking a position on, the merits of what one hears and by not becoming so immersed in the situation that the counselor loses a sense of his or her own objective view.

Feelings are at the heart of counseling; they are the material with which the counselor works. What are feelings, and why are they important? The word "feeling" is interesting in itself; it has a transitive and an intransitive meaning. There is "feeling" as in touching something, and there is "feeling" as in being touched. A feeling, then, for the purposes of this definition, is that which is evoked in a person, when a particular event, either real or imagined, touches some vital part of that person, and arouses a response from within.

There is a basic repertoire of feelings which every human being experiences in some way, and the early traces of these appear in infancy and childhood. The feelings that emerge in counseling—loneliness, sadness, anger, guilt, and other such—are versions of and variations on experiences known in some form throughout life. The work of counseling, then, is to reach out toward the infant, the child, the person inside the student, to honor that basic human repertoire of feelings, and to acknowledge the intensity, the forms and shapes those feelings take. It is those feelings which must be respected and understood and which a counselor comes to see in each person he or she deals with in a unique and complicated array, never to be seen again in the same fashion in anyone else.

Feelings in children and adolescents are often extremely intense, and they are sometimes experienced as commands. People in the grip of intense feelings sometimes feel compelled to act on them. They do not feel that they have choices or really have control over or responsibility for what they do. Listening to one's own feelings, recognizing them as feelings and not as commands, and learning to express them in various modes other than action constitute an important developmental task that starts in childhood and continues throughout life.

Growth, then, has a special meaning in counseling. The kind of growth the counselor seeks to foster involves the bringing of feelings into focus, the gradual maturing of feelings, and the bringing of feelings into a kind of reconciliation with the limits and disappointments of life. Growth in this sense is not the same as adapting or conforming in life or becoming what others require one to be. Growth means learning more fully about oneself and, in so doing, reducing the potential of feelings to become incapacitating in some way, as they tend to do when feelings are too intense or when they exist in conflict with each other. Growth also involves learning enough about one's feelings to know when or when not to act on them, to make choices about one's actions, and take responsibility for them. Self-discovery of this kind is, of itself, a maturing and therapeutic process.

Adolescence is a particularly good time to begin to encourage this kind of self-discovery. As Piaget and the cognitive development theorists have shown, adolescence is the first stage in which people have the cognitive capacity to reflect on their inner experiences and to think about feelings. It is partly for this reason that the Counseling Institutes focus primarily on adolescents and adolescent development, since it is a developmental period at which people are discovering the nature of feelings and may be especially inclined to talk about them.

The Development of Self-Esteem

Self-esteem is something usually either absent or reduced in students who seek counseling and something which counseling aims to help restore. Healthy self-esteem in this sense means that they accept themselves, like themselves, and want to go on being who they are, while at the same time being able to acknowledge their flaws and limitations.

For most of us, self-esteem is derived from a number of sources, perhaps the most important of which is our relationships with other people. The ability to have satisfying relationships, to be oneself in the company of another, and to enjoy another person's company, is often missing in people who seek counseling. Sometimes the relationship with a counselor is the first opportunity a person has to experience this kind of close contact with another. Its artificially constructed one-sidedness makes it an unusual sort of relationship in someone's life, of course, but that also makes it safe—safe from another's demands or needs and, for the time being, safe enough to explore one's own experiences in that relationship. The work of counseling, hopefully, paves the way for other, more symmetrical and spontaneous relationships in the student's life.

Rules of the Counseling Relationship

In the long run, we hope that various relationships in the student's life will contain the elements that are—or should be—present in the counseling relationship. We hope they will have relationships in which their feelings are heard and respected, in which they can grow and learn about themselves, and in which they can build self-esteem and feel connected in a close way to the other person. But, in the meantime, it is the *safety* of the counseling relationship which makes it special and makes those experiences possible. There are certain principles or ground rules that apply to the counseling relationship which, taken together, make it safe and permit the counseling work to occur.

The four principles which follow can be adhered to in the professional counseling relationship but only with somewhat more difficulty in the teacher/student counseling relationship. They are presented, therefore, with the caveat that they need to be developed and shaped in a way that is suitable to the community in which the teacher and the student find themselves. They should be understood, nevertheless, as representing standards to approach as closely as possible when counseling is being practiced.

First, the student should be guaranteed the protection of complete confidentiality. Assurance should be given that what is said will not be repeated to anyone else, with only two exceptions. The most important one occurs when a student reveals that his or her life, or someone else's life, is in danger. In those cases the counselor must protect life over confidentiality and alert anyone who can assist in that effort. The other exception occurs in learning and training situations when the counselor discusses ongoing work with a consultant, who is also bound to respect the confidential nature of the material.

Second, the counselor should maintain a neutral or non-judgmental attitude toward the feelings and the behavior of the student. Rather than judging the student, the counselor should work to understand feelings and behavior and, in particular, to understand what they mean *to the student*. It is the judgment of the student about himself or herself that is the significant matter, and students must be assured that their judgment will not be crowded out by the counselor's judgment and that the conversation will not become adversarial.

In thinking about this neutrality principle, it is useful also to make a distinction between judging a student as a person—his or her style, values, or opinions—and judging the student's behavior. There are times when it is important for the counselor to express a judgment, as in situations when a student's behavior is offensive or provocative in some way. In these situations the counselor walks a thin line, trying to avoid condemning the student as a person, but making it clear that certain kinds of behavior are unacceptable. A teacher who is angry at a student who has behaved offensively sometimes has to take a deep breath, try to suspend judgment of the student as a person, and look for a constructive way to talk with the student about the behavior.

Third, the counseling relationship must be non-exploitive. This means that it exists to meet the needs of the student, not the counselor. Students must be assured that what they say will not in some way be used against them, and that the counselor will not take advantage of their trust and the state of vulnerability which may transiently accompany the counseling work. A counselor must understand that the slightest suggestion on his or her part is likely to be perceived by the student as a command, even when it is not intended as such. Students who seek counseling often do so because they cannot or do not make their own decisions. Sometimes they do not even know what they want from themselves or their families, or even from life. A counselor therefore must always guard against the temptation to abuse a certain inequality, which invariably exists in the relationship, to serve his or her own needs.

Fourth, the counselor should have a non-authoritarian relationship with the student. By this we mean that a counselor should not tell the student what to do, how to behave, or, most importantly, how to feel. Thus, the counselor does not generally give advice or solve problems for the student. The solutions to problems in the student's life ultimately must come from the student. The work of counseling is to uncover or develop those solutions from the framework of the student's life, not from the assumptions or expectations of the counselor.

We have found over the years that the message implicit in this last principle is one of the hardest for teachers to put into practice. Many teachers are problem-solvers by nature. When they see something not working, they try to fix it. In a lecture she has given on counseling, Dr. Janet Sand offers the following advice to a teacher-counselor struggling against the impulse to intervene and take over for a student: "Don't just do something. Stand there."

These four principles define a special and safe relationship in which counseling can occur. But the counseling relationship sometimes has elements of other kinds of relationships in it. Sometimes it overlaps with other relationships and sometimes it is confused with other kinds of relationships. Accordingly it is important to make some distinctions that further clarify what counseling is and what it is not. This is particularly important when counseling is being practiced in the rather informal and spontaneous ways that are likely in schools and when the person doing the counseling also has other roles in the student's life.

Counseling vs. Advising

An important distinction to be made between counseling and advising was alluded to in the explanation of the fourth principle. More clarification is necessary, however, particularly since much of the counseling done in schools occurs between designated "advisers" and "advisees." Advising is usually considered a kind of problem-solving activity, in which the absence of information is causing a problem and the adviser's access to information can help bring about a solution to the problem. Advisers are assigned to students for this reason. They possess information and a certain kind of power in the community which the student lacks. An adviser can decide that a student's academic problems could be solved by changing classes, waiving an academic requirement or something of the sort, and then take action to bring about the solution.

Most problems that arise in schools are dealt with in this way. As mentioned earlier, it is natural for teachers to take an active, interventionist role and to feel that the most helpful thing they can do for the student is to solve the problem so that he or she can move on. In some situations that is, indeed, the appropriate approach. However, it is likely to put the student in the position of being a passive partner in decisions being made about him or her. While this approach may be more efficient than having the student participate in the decision, it can also represent a lost opportunity for the student to take over some of the responsibility of decision making.

Additionally, any experienced adviser knows that there are some situations in which none of the "fix-it" solutions seem to be effective. Sometimes repeated attempts are made to solve problems, but new problems keep cropping up. When this happens, the adviser may rightly conclude that he or she does not understand what the problem is, since none of the usual remedies have helped. Often this feeling of bafflement—having run out of tricks—is the adviser's first clue that counseling, and not advising, is needed.

Counseling is a kind of problem solving in which a lack of information, or facts, or power is not the problem. But feelings are the issue, and it is the student who possesses that information. Feelings can produce problems in self-esteem, problems in behavior and in relationships, and problems in performance. The work of counseling is to identify and work with the student's feelings.

The counseling relationship therefore is more of a collaboration than that of the adviser and advisee. The solutions that emerge grow out of the student's willingness to share information about feelings, and the counselor's willingness to listen and understand. There should be a mutual sense of responsibility for any action that occurs as a result of the work done.

Counseling vs. Friendship

The distinctions between the counseling relationship and friendship are in some ways obvious and in other ways subtle. In the professional counseling relationship there is usually the understanding that no efforts should be made to pursue social contact, as friends would. This limit is not as easy to observe in the counseling relationships in schools, and it is probably not as sacred a rule as it is sometimes thought to be.

Other aspects of friendship, however, really do have no place in the counseling relationship. To some extent many friendships, like many marriages, depend on a tacit mutual agreement not to push painful confrontation concerning personal issues on one another. Unless there is a deep crisis in the relationship, there is usually an understanding and acceptance—reflecting an investment in each other, as is—and a reluctance by one partner to rock the boat by touching on sensitive feelings in the other. A counselor's role is to accept the student as is, but also to risk arousing some angry and negative feelings for the sake of looking at issues that the student may not be comfortable with. A counselor has to risk not being liked at times—a risk that many friends are not willing to take with each other.

To some extent too, friends tend to look for some congruence of values in each other, or at least something in the other that matches needs of one's own. The principle of neutrality makes this aspect of friendship something which a counselor must try to avoid. In order to understand fully the nature of another person's experience, one has to renounce an investment in the outcome of the counseling encounter or in what one discovers in the course of the counseling dialogue. Many people who seek counseling think that their friends would be disappointed if they really found out who they were. The counselor should permit the student to explore himself or herself as fully as possible in a climate in which their relationship is not hanging in the balance. The other side of this coin, of course, is that the counselor should not be seeking friends through counseling, but should find ways to meet those personal needs in his or her other relationships.

Counseling vs. Parenting

Counseling, particularly with children and adolescents, sometimes arouses parental feelings. Accordingly, the distinctions between counseling and parenting—though on some level obvious—still need to be spelled out. These distinctions are particularly relevant in schools, especially boarding schools, where in many cases teacher/counselors see a great deal more of the students they work with than their parents do and sometimes have a quasi-parental role in the students' lives.

The main distinction to be drawn between parenting and counseling has to do with the inevitable narcissistic fantasies that can dominate a parent's view of his or her child. These wishes are often expressed in demands they make on their children, quite unconsciously, to become certain kinds of people. At some point most children rebel, a little bit at least, against these fantasies and demands. Most also worry that they will lose their parents' love if the sense they have of themselves does not correspond to what the parents want or expect. Achieving a sense of oneself—an identity and some notion of what one is becoming—is a primary task in adolescence. Adolescents need support from a neutral party when they begin to struggle with the dilemma of wanting to retain ties to their parents and, at the same time, wanting to become themselves. At these times, a counselor who is definitely not a parent can be of enormous help.

Teacher/counselors who grow attached to students are in some danger of building their own set of fantasies—and some implied expectations, too—and they have to work to minimize those feelings if they want to become effective counselors. They must work against the natural impulse to become a surrogate parent for the student. It is one thing for a counselor to come to understand a student's belief that his or her parents have failed in some way, but it is much more problematic if the counselor accepts that judgment and proceeds to act on it by trying to fill the gap. Becoming a substitute parent, when one decides that the student has inadequate ones at home, only postpones an important piece of work in the student's life, and it also leaves the student vulnerable to more disappointment. One of the primary tasks in development is coming to terms with what one was given in the way of parents. A counselor's efforts to replace a student's parents is sometimes an expression of the counselor's failure to resolve that problem in his or her own life, and they can in fact interfere with the growth of the student. Also, a teacher or counselor cannot realistically make a lifelong commitment to a student and in the long run is bound to regret becoming overinvolved in this way. Relationships of this kind, in which the teacher has tried to rescue a student from difficulties in his or her life, usually sour over time, leaving both people with a feeling of loss and disappointment. This disappointment can be avoided if the teacher/counselor keeps in mind the reality of the relationship and respects realistic boundaries and limits.

Techniques in Counseling

Some of the techniques used in counseling help to define it as its own kind of activity; thus, a review of those techniques is an important part of an effort to define counseling. It is equally important, however, to bear in mind that the experienced counselor's technique is almost invisible. It is not technique but the *person* of the counselor, his or her particular style with people, and his or her feelings for the student and reactions to the student that constitute the moving force in the relationship. Although a review of technique might leave the impression that the counselor-student relationship is rather impersonal, it is anything but that. Both people bring their own personalities, their own styles, their own feelings to the relationship, and those are the distinguishing features of the relationship far more than technique.

Technique, then, as we understand it, really involves a set of guide-

lines for counselors, around which they try to structure their half of
the counseling dialogue. There is no one way to do counseling in any
situation. There are no recipes for a successful counseling session.
And, in a sense, since this is a human relationship, there is no way to
"master" the technique. Counselors work in a new medium every
time they begin with a different student. Technique therefore is always being adapted and changed to meet the needs of the relationship and to further the process of counseling. Following are five
aspects of what we loosely call counseling technique: (1) listening, (2)
encouraging ventilation, (3) clarification, (4) interpretation, and (5)
support.

1. *Listening is the most important aspect of technique.* The counselor listens on many levels to what the student says—listening to the
words and their connotations and nuances, to the feelings behind the
words, to the figures of speech, to the tone of the student's voice, and
to the silences, when the student seems unable or unwilling to talk.
In other words, the counselor listens for the full meaning and all the
separate meanings of what is being expressed, and is always asking,
"What am I really hearing? What is this person trying to tell me?"
Until the counselor gets some idea of what that meaning is, he or she
says very little to the student except words to encourage the student
to go on talking.

The quality of a silence is something to which a counselor listens
too, and this is a very difficult part of technique for inexperienced
counselors. If the counselor is paying attention and does not interrupt
the silence prematurely, he or she will notice that it has a meaning
with some relation to what has been said so far, such as "there is no
more to say," or "I can't find the words to say what I am feeling," or
"It has been a relief to get that off my chest."

Silences are likely to make inexperienced counselors anxious. They
tend to feel that they should be doing something or saying something
to fill the gap. Sometimes they experience the silence as a subtle
challenge or criticism on the student's part. Whatever the meaning
of a silence, however, the important thing is to understand it, not to
react to it or interrupt it. And so, in the process of learning to be
more effective, counselors should practice sitting through silences,
hopefully growing less uncomfortable with them and gradually coming to understand and respect the meaning a silence may have.

2. *"Ventilation" is the technical term for talking or letting off
steam, which is what the counselor tries to facilitate in the student.*

Techniques of encouraging ventilation are crucial to counseling, because the dialogue depends on the student's speaking freely and honestly and from the heart. In a variety of ways the counselor creates an atmosphere in which the student comes to feel heard and understood and accepted. In that situation the student will usually begin to reveal strong feelings about sensitive matters, often feelings which he or she does not discuss with other people but which urgently need attention. A counselor must show and sustain genuine interest and demonstrate a capacity to hear the student out and must not judge or react immediately but continue to listen and try to understand what the student is saying.

The technique of encouraging ventilation also lies in the counselor's ability to sense those things which probably involve strong feelings in the student but which may not initially appear to be that important. For example, after hearing that a student who is in some academic difficulty has just returned from visiting his father in the hospital, the counselor might ask how the visit went for him and pursue it a little further, perhaps, even though it appears that the student is not aware of the experience having affected him. With experience, counselors develop a sixth sense for feelings that are hidden in the student and develop the skill to help the student express them as they begin to surface.

3. *A counselor tries to clarify what he or she is hearing on a number of levels.* Sometimes a story comes out very jumbled, with facts so intermixed with strong feelings that the account is as confusing to the counselor as to the student. A counselor must, of course, understand the information well enough to be oriented to the student's situation. Beyond that, though, the counselor tries to clarify what is said, for himself or herself and for the student by getting at and identifying the feelings associated with the story. Clarification in counseling means taking what one hears and sorting it into a manageable set of ideas, labeling feelings, putting words around experiences, and making elusive or unspoken feelings accessible to thought and available for discussion. When it is effective, clarification does not put distance between the counselor and what is said—as in, "I hear you saying you feel some hostility toward your parents." Instead, it involves learning to use language that is very close to feelings, bringing them into closer range where they can be felt by both the counselor and the student—as in, "You sound very angry at your parents."

A good job of clarification can sometimes reveal to the student paradoxes of feelings, or conflicts, or ambivalence—as when a counselor points out that the student seems to be angry but is also afraid to hurt his or her parents. Conflicting or ambivalent feelings make people feel very stuck and are often difficult to identify, because they manifest themselves in obscure ways. Over time the clarification of conflicting feelings and the opportunity to talk them out permits the student who feels stuck or emotionally paralyzed to begin to move forward.

4. *Interpretation is an aspect of technique which has a slightly different meaning in the counseling situation than it does in the more formal psychotherapeutic setting.* In the latter, the therapist uses interpretation to draw connections between feelings and behavior and unconscious or preconscious motivation. In that situation, the therapist draws his or her interpretation from a number of sources, including what the patient talks about directly and indirectly and the therapist's theory of motivation. In the counseling situation, on the other hand, interpretation is a more informal kind of activity, drawn from the counselor's sense of what may be going on that the student does not see. An interpretation in this sense is more of a tentative hypothesis—an attempt to suggest an explanation, usually put in the form of a question to the student, such as, "Do you think there might be some connection between the trouble you are having getting your work done and the fact that your father has been ill?" The counselor may offer a hunch, with the clear implication that the student need not accept it as valid explanation. In this sense, again, the counseling relationship involves collaboration, working together to build a shared interpretation or understanding of the causes and the meaning of the student's experience.

5. *As a technique, support in the counseling relationship is, in general, expressed passively, more often in things the counselor does not say, than in things he or she does say.* The counselor tries to refrain from making direct reassuring statements, such as, "Don't worry. I am sure everything will be all right." Comments like this are sometimes reassuring to the counselor who may be worried about the student, but they are almost never reassuring to the student, who has no reason to believe that the counselor knows how difficult the situation is. A good supportive statement to a worried student is something like, "I can see how worried you are. This must be very difficult for you. Would you like to talk more about it?" The direct acknowl-

edgment of feelings and the offer of help with those feelings is very reassuring to someone who feels alone and overwhelmed.

Listening, talking with and caring enough about someone really to understand him or her is, in itself, supportive. But there are also some situations in which the counselor is in a position to identify strengths in the student—strengths which the student may not have fully acknowledged to himself or herself—and to help the student begin to use them. For example, a counselor might say to a student, "You have been able to tell me recently what you feel you need from your parents and how you feel about what they have been doing. Maybe soon you will feel able to begin talking with them." Active support in the counseling relationship does not mean doing something *for* the student; it involves encouraging the student to do something for himself or herself, but doing that only when the student finds it realistically possible. When the task of making a change feels overwhelming to the student, it is sometimes the counselor's belief in the student that helps him or her get started and eventually bring that change to pass. In the long run, support is less an aspect of technique than it is an aspect of the counseling *relationship*, whether it is being expressed directly or indirectly.

When to Counsel

In what situations, then, is it appropriate for teachers to do counseling? In the following chapter, Dr. Stanley King discusses the kinds of counseling that are appropriate in schools. For the purposes of this discussion of definition and philosophy, it is useful to describe some generic types of situations and to clarify the role of counseling in the school setting. As we try to emphasize at the Northfield–Fountain Valley Counseling Institutes, we make no attempt to train teachers to be either professional diagnosticians or professional therapists. Nevertheless, we believe strongly that there is a clear place for counseling activities to go on in teacher/student relationships. We believe, further, that there is good reason for teachers to have some familiarity with overall psychological assessment, so that they are equipped to distinguish those situations which call for attention. The Counseling Institutes maintain that these are appropriate professional skills for teachers to acquire, since they have so much day-to-day contact with students and play such an important part in students' lives.

Most of the counseling work that teachers should be doing involves *normal* developmental processes in children and adolescents. Certain kinds of difficulties—such as academic slumps, some acting out, ambivalence and conflict, and stress in relationships or work—are normal parts of human growth. Sensitive counseling intervention during those periods can help the student to resolve them more quickly or prevent them from becoming more seriously dysfunctional. Just as important, however, we stress that these periods also represent opportunities for personal growth and the development of self-understanding, particularly during adolescence. One of the most important lessons of the Counseling Institutes, and a lesson that we try to convey to the Institute participants on many levels, is that this growth of self-knowledge has a crucial place in the overall educational process.

How, then, how does a teacher or adviser identify a problem in a student that suggests that counseling is needed? Ordinarily, students do not present themselves at teachers' offices with clear requests for help, as patients or clients do with the professional therapist. Students are more likely to indicate that they are in difficulty by less direct means. To a certain extent their behavior may reveal their difficulty, as will be described, but their failure to respond to the usual remedies also tells us they need help. Schools have tremendously varied repertoires of solutions to problems that children present. After all, the business of education involves figuring out needs of individual children and groups of children and developing programs to suit those needs. But certain children seem not to be able to use the means available to them to move forward in their lives. They get stuck, and then they stay stuck. Furthermore, patterns of maladaptive behavior usually emerge gradually over time. As described earlier, typically schools attempt many solutions with such students. And also, typically, many solutions (and advisers) fail. This is the indirect route many people travel toward getting help, but it is almost universally the route children and adolescents take. The teacher/counselor therefore has to bear in mind that, by the time it is clear that a student needs counseling, a sense of helplessness and failure has already developed, probably in both the teacher and the student, as well as in the parents.

There are several types of situations which commonly arise in schools and which teachers should be alert to as potentially calling for counseling. The first involves a student who repeatedly breaks rules in the school, bringing trouble on himself and perhaps on the community. Along with whatever disciplinary action is taken, at some point there needs to be an exploration of the student's feelings about himself or herself, about the school, about his or her behavior, about his or her relationships. Many such students have no desire to leave the school; for them, expulsion would represent failure on everybody's part, including their own. In some cases the behavior involves an effort to express feelings of being misunderstood and a wish for some attention to be paid to the frustrations and unhappiness which are the underlying causes of the behavior. Students sometimes have a great deal of difficulty in articulating feelings of this kind directly, if at all. Some such situations call for professional help; some require withdrawal from the school. Other students can be helped significantly by an informal, personal, on-going counseling relationship with a teacher, dean, or other adult in the community. In these instances the focus of the school's attention can turn from the effects of the behavior, which have caused everybody so much concern, to the meaning of the behavior, which is the real concern of the student. Understanding what the behavior means can go a long way to helping a student decide whether or not to continue engaging in it.

A second example is the depressed student, one who seems to feel chronically low or fatigued, who perhaps does not have very many friends, and whose academic or athletic performance does not match his or her assumed or previously demonstrated capabilities. The many signs that lead one to think that a student might be depressed are discussed in Chapter 10. Counseling is needed when those signs have begun to accumulate. At this point, an interested adviser, coach, or teacher should sit down with the student, state what it is they are concerned may be going on, and encourage the student to begin talking about how he or she has been feeling.

A third example involves a student who shows a marked drop in academic performance over a period of time. Shifts are sometimes gradual and imperceptible, but school records show these shifts if they are there. Sometimes depression is involved in a drop in performance, and sometimes there may be situational causes. Whatever the reason, the matter should be taken up with the student, who is probably troubled, too, by his or her falling grades and needs to understand its causes if he or she is going to bring them under control.

A fourth example is a student who copes well—perhaps too well—with a serious loss or change in his or her personal life. Unlike the student whose performance declines as a result of circumstances in his or her life, this student bears up, shows little reaction, and goes on as if he or she was not affected. All too often people around such students admire the student's maturity and are grateful not to have to deal with any acute reaction that the student might be undergoing. The absence of an emotional reaction to loss, death, divorce, illness or any such experience is at least as serious, if not more so, than most overt reactions, and it should be attended to. Sometimes students feel they have to protect others in their family or are uncomfortable about revealing what they consider to be private business without having appropriate permission from their family. Still others feel it is not acceptable to show feelings about these events. An interested teacher/counselor can provide a key outlet at a time when students let their need for privacy override their need for support and help. A tactful and understanding counselor can help a student express some of the painful feelings behind the cool facade and help prevent a deepening and more insidious emotional knot from developing.

Opportunities for counseling students appear in many forms. This list is only the briefest of generic samples. The important factor is always the interest on the part of the adults in the community, their "radar" for feelings in students, and their courage to take the risk of inquiring when nothing actually is the matter. Teachers frequently underestimate the healing power of even the briefest, simplest counseling interventions. Many make those interventions instinctively, sometimes without being particularly aware that they are doing counseling. Just as many shy away from making them for fear of intruding, for fear of not being able to fix the problem, or for fear of not having the answers. Other fears enter in, too: "I'm not qualified to handle these things." "The student will become too dependent on me." "How can I possibly do more than I am already doing?" "There is no time in the schedule, or place, where I can talk to a student privately." These are all valid, real concerns. In some schools there is the very confusing reality of a schedule that denies people any free time—a climate that appears to value hard work, competition, and a hard-nosed approach to individual problems—and, on the other hand, an administration that sends people year after year to the Northfield-Fountain Valley Counseling Institutes to learn how to counsel students.

These ambiguities and contradictions exist in most schools, and they leave teachers unclear about what is expected of them as teacher/counselors. It is the goal of the Northfield and Fountain Valley Counseling Institutes to focus on counseling opportunities and to look at the obstacles to counseling that the teacher faces, but then to go on to explore what may be going on in the student who is having difficulty and in the teacher who wants to help. In the relaxing and supportive atmosphere of the Institutes there is an opportunity to pursue these questions in real depth. The result of the Institute experience for many is that there develops a sharpening of teachers' awareness, a honing of skills, and often a greater confidence on the part of the teacher to try counseling and a willingness to overcome some of the obstacles. Over the years there has grown in the Institute faculty a clearer definition of the type of counseling that teachers can do, a deepened respect for the complexity of the job of teachers, and an admiration for many of the people who take it on.

Chapter 2

COUNSELING ON THE RUN

Stanley H. King

The image evoked by the title of this chapter is one of hurry, limited contact between people, and pressure of time—certainly not a picture of leisure. A central fact we have learned from teachers is the reality of the time demands of everyday life in both day and boarding schools. Any counseling between teacher and student almost invariably has to be done within time constraints. At the same time we have learned of the special quality of relationships that exist between teachers and students in most independent schools. These relationships are made possible by small classes, the involvement of teachers in activities outside the classroom, and the commitment by schools to the education of the total person—social and moral as well as intellectual. As a result, there can be an enhancing of the brief encounters between teachers and students when counseling takes place. We have learned, in short, that counseling on the run is a viable concept, that it rests on the same premises as the more formal counseling process, and that it can be effective. Perhaps the most important lesson from Northfield and Fountain Valley is that teachers with little or no training in counseling procedures can learn to do counseling on the run, or at least learn its principles in a relatively short time and reinforce the learning by practice throughout the school year.

We know that the idea of counseling students makes some teachers uneasy. They usually feel that they are not equipped by training or temperament to help students with emotional problems. Sometimes they say that they do not like to intrude in personal matters or to invade privacy, or they are apprehensive that they will incur the displeasure of parents if the student should reveal information or feelings about the family to the teacher. Others are reluctant to "stir things up," fearful that if strong feelings are expressed, if emotional conflicts appear, or if the student feels stuck in making decisions or taking action, they will be beyond their depth and not know what to do. At other times, teachers express the fear that they will make a mistake if they intervene as counselors and harm the student in some manner. These fears are understandable, and we appreciate their impact on teachers. However, our experience at Northfield and Fountain Valley is that such fears are often exaggerated, and that teachers can quickly learn their limits and how to work effectively within those limits. As a beginning then, consider a vignette.

Working within Limits

Gerald is a sophomore in a boarding school, and you happen to be his adviser. One afternoon he comes to your room just as you are ready to leave for soccer practice. He says that he is having difficulty in his European history course. He notes that the teacher has been unfair in grading tests and, furthermore, makes sarcastic remarks about Gerald's comments in class discussions. Gerald says, rather angrily, that he is at the top of the teacher's "fecal roster" and he doesn't like it one bit. You happen to know that this particular teacher has a reputation for making cutting remarks in the classroom. Gerald wants you, as his adviser, to do something about his complaints. You are pushed for time in an already busy day and are not exactly certain about how to respond to Gerald.

This scenario is familiar to most teachers, whether they are in day or boarding schools, as is the question of how to respond. Usually these situations call for—or might call for—a counseling approach, and they often turn up when the teacher (coach, adviser, dorm parent) least expects them, is unprepared, or has other matters demanding attention. Sometimes they occur when the teacher is fatigued from the attrition of a long day or a wearying academic term. In short, counseling situations not infrequently come at inopportune times. To the student, however, the matter is usually pressing and at the forefront of his or her attention. Gerald could probably think of little else when he came to your room in the dormitory, his focus being moti-vated—at least on a conscious level—by his anger at the unfairness of it all.

Potential counseling situations also occur in places that are inap-propriate for good counseling interactions. If you had been Gerald's teacher, you would have been fortunate because he came to your room where you had the opportunity for some privacy. More often something happens in the classroom: a student bursts out crying; you are approached in the hallway of a classroom building or outside the door to the library reading room by a student who says, "I've got to talk to you!"; two students stop you as you pass their table in the din-ing hall and tell you they're worried about a roommate; or you walk off the soccer field toward the locker room and a player says that her English teacher asked her to talk to you, her adviser. These situations commonly take place in public with other students around and often where there is no privacy or even a place to sit down together.

One of the first and most important lessons we learned from teach-ers is the substantial difference in the setting in which counseling in-teractions take place between the teacher/counselor and the professional therapist. The latter's opportunities for doing counseling seem luxurious by comparison. Therapists work in a private office that is virtually soundproof and protected from the interruptions of visitors or telephone calls. There is an allotted time—usually 50 min-utes—so that the people who come for help have an opportunity to compose themselves before they leave if they have been upset. Fur-thermore, there is not only more time, but the therapist has greater opportunity to think about the counseling interaction as it is taking place, to monitor it, and to reflect on his/her own feelings about the material presented by the patient. There is also an opportunity to ex-plore side issues, to plumb the depth of feelings, and to recover from missed opportunities in the counseling interaction.

Despite these advantages, our experience through the two Insti-tutes has taught us that the basic approach that we use in the con-sulting room can be utilized in a modified form in the brief and often infrequent interactions that teachers have with students. The atti-tude and the techniques, the essential nature of the counseling re-lationship, are similar in counseling on the run and therapy in the consulting room. Wtih some practice and some experience, teachers can bring a counseling approach to bear on most of their short-term contacts with students. That approach is remarkably effective in facilitating the resolution of students' problems.

Consider another scenario. Janice is a junior, a rather quiet and attractive person who does not stand out in the crowd. She does not seem to have many friends, but at the same time, she does not strike you as a loner. She has a part in the spring musical and you are the teacher responsible for coordinating the work in this production. Janice has been late for a few rehearsals recently and you have noticed that she looks a little tense at times. You get into a conversation with her after a rehearsal, in the course of which you ask her if everything is all right and how things are with her friends. As the two of you talk she seems nervous, especially when you ask about her close girl friends. Suddenly she blurts out, "Do you think I'm a lesbian?"

Janice, like Gerald, poses a question that demands a response—at least, the teacher is likely to feel such a demand, especially under the conditions of time and place noted above. The almost automatic response of the teacher is likely to be affected by the wish to be a problem solver, to fix things and clear up misunderstandings, and above all to make the situation better. The teacher will think of what needs to be done, how the situation can be corrected, what information to supply to the student, or how to reroute his feelings into safe areas. But to act on that impulse is to intervene with the student in a way that may defeat a basic purpose of counseling—namely, to facilitate problem solving in the student. The struggle to avoid "rescuing" people in trouble is common and persistent among all caretakers, counselors, and therapists, and teacher/counselors may have significant difficulty overcoming that need, especially at the beginning.

In the Institutes at Northfield and Fountain Valley, much of the teaching takes place in small group meetings and in the role-playing of student and teacher problem situations. In the first days of each Institute it is common that the person assuming the role of teacher will respond as a problem solver, putting emphasis on the behavioral facts that the student presents or asking questions of the student in that mode. Only over the course of a week—and with signal dependence on role playing—do teachers begin to feel comfortable with a different kind of initial and continuing response.

An Essential Ingredient: Listening

The counseling approach requires that the teacher resist the "fix it" response and *listen* to what the student is trying to say. What one does initially to facilitate listening can be very simple, ranging from looking attentive but saying nothing, to "Oh?", to "Tell me more." In the situations with Gerald and Janice there is a considerable pressure of feelings on the part of the student, and this is usually the case when a student comes to you. Hence, a limited but attentive response will help the student say more.

As noted in the definition of counseling in Chapter 1, listening is the first aspect of the counseling process. Basically it is an active, not a passive procedure. It is more easily accomplished if the teacher has in mind trying to identify the real issues on the student's mind—that is, real issues in terms of feelings. Listening gives the student time to provide material that can help the teacher work at the cognitive task of deciding what the student's dominant feelings are. But listening is more than just a playing for time: it shifts the focus of the interaction more directly to the student and makes the student the more active participant and the teacher the more passive. That subtle shift in focus, which is largely under the control of the teacher, is central to the counseling approach. Although the teacher may be passive in the interaction, he or she will be active cognitively, sorting through possibilities of what may be going on in the student's mind and thinking about what to say that can bring about a fuller expression of the student's feelings. With Janice, the teacher might respond initially with "Oh?", then as Jancie continued the teacher might well say, "This certainly seems upsetting to you. Can you tell me more?"

These brief responses are facilitated by a facial expression and body language that underscore the shift in focus to the student: body turned toward the student, eyes on her face, a receptive stance. We may not be aware of how much is conveyed in human interaction through facial expression and body language, especially in the way one person regards another. If you are talking to someone at a party, and that person is looking all around the room while you talk, you may well have the feeling that this person does not care much about what you are saying—or perhaps about you. On the positive side, body language can connote attentiveness, and attentiveness can help the expression of feelings. Conversely, body language on the part of the student can provide important information for the teacher in discerning what is going on with the student. The agitation and tension probably evident in Janice would be further reason for the teacher to say that Janice seemed upset.

The focus of the listening, then, is on feelings, as evident in what the student says and reveals by body language. This kind of listening takes vigilance, because the feelings may be embedded in a flow of words about events, people, and abstract thoughts. Words that connote feeling may be present, protruding slightly from the surrounding matrix, or the feelings may be disguised, available only to the "third ear" of the teacher—that is, only implied in the thoughts or by certain behavior on the part of the student, or in the interaction that the student describes with another person. Disguised feelings are easy to miss when other kinds of material in the student's presentation seem to dominate and the teacher gets caught up in the questions of: Who? What? Where? When? and Why?

But if the teacher listens actively rather than talking too much, there is opportunity to concentrate on the flow of words by the student and pick out the indicators of emotions. The teacher may only want to make note of this for the moment, at least, while allowing the student to talk further. At some point the teacher will want to respond to the feelings, to resonate with them, to reflect them. The response to Janice, "This certainly seems upsetting to you," is an example of resonating or reflecting of feelings. With Gerald, the response might be, "You sound pretty angry and as though you felt really put down." The first part of this statement is evident from Gerald's words, his tone of voice, and, likely, his posture. The latter part of the statement is an inference from Gerald's words, based on what most of us feel when others make sarcastic remarks about us. If you have to put Gerald off until later due to the pressure of time, you will at least have left him with the understanding that you have paid attention to one of the most important things on his mind—his anger. If he is to sort out his problem in some manner with you, that common understanding will help in forming a working relationship.

The Need to Remain Neutral

Another aspect of listening as an active process is the necessity to suspend judgment. One does not hear as well if one is judging things as they are said. A judgment may have to do with what the teacher already knows or feels about the student. With Gerald it might be based on whether the teacher likes him or not, whether Gerald has been in trouble before, or how the teacher feels about the colleague whom Gerald dislikes. The inclination toward judgment—being judgmental, as it is commonly referred to—may also come from the way Gerald presents his case, enhanced by the fact that he is bothering the teacher at an inopportune time. In the case of Janice, the teacher may have some personal reactions to the idea of homosexuality or worries about it, or have positive or negative feelings about it that could affect her response in a judgmental way. The very notion may be so threatening that the teacher will try to get rid of Janice as quickly as possible and not want to hear any more about it. Suspending judgment has to be a conscious action within the teacher's own mind—an active process. In carrying out this sometimes difficult task, the teacher may be helped by differentiating in his or her own mind between making a judgment about something the student says or does, on the one hand, and what or who the student is, on the other hand. Problems of being judgmental often arise from confusing the nature of the behavior from how the student is valued in the teacher's mind.

Clearly, the suspending of judgment depends on the ability to monitor one's own feelings. None of us hears what the other person is saying as well if we let anger, anxiety, sexual interest, or other feelings get in the way. An example from my own clinical experience can illustrate the point. I had been working with a young man, a student in college, for awhile, and felt that we were developing a good relationship. I had a session with him in early summer, shortly after I had purchased a new madras sport jacket, and I wore it to the session. I happen to be red-green color blind and usually make certain that I take my wife with me on clothes shopping expeditions. This time I had not done so, and in truth the jacket was a bit garish. My patient looked at me and said, "Where did you get that jacket?" in a tone that suggested disapproval or doubt about my taste in clothes. I passed it off lightly and the session began. After about ten minutes I realized that I was responding to my patient in a sharp manner, with some edge to my voice. Wondering why, to myself, made me aware of my anger at his remark and probably at myself for not being more careful about my purchase. I told him about this and apologized for my insensitivity. We were then able to talk about the effect of all this on our working relationship and the therapy could proceed.

Feelings on the part of the teacher that can impede the listening process may arise from the student's words, actions, or appearance, or they can come from the teacher's own life experience. A teacher preoccupied with personal problems in a relationship, frustrated by a partner's or colleague's actions, or ruminating about failure or rejection will find it more difficult to hear what a student is trying to say and to correctly identify his or her feelings. In counseling on the run—in the active listening process—the teacher must monitor his or her own feelings and try to gauge how those feelings might affect a response to the student. Once again, the monitoring of the teacher's own feelings makes the listening an active process. Let me illustrate this in a different way. If a student talks to you about a sexual matter or is concerned about sexual behavior, or the consequences of it, you may be tempted to ask questions about the details of the sexual behavior rather than the feelings of the student about it. This is not unusual because most of us have a natural interest in sexual behavior and curiosity about it. But indulging that interest or curiosity can impede listening for the feelings of the student. The teacher will also have attitudes or values about sexuality that can get in the way, as I suggested in how the teacher might respond to Janice.

The teacher's feelings are discussed at greater length in Chapter 4. Suffice to say here that emphasis must be placed on the importance of self-knowledge by the teacher—knowledge about how he or she is feeling at the moment and is likely to react in the face of certain situations or certain behaviors by students. Such self-knowledge can help the teacher to filter out dysfunctional and other distracting private or personal matters and to listen more effectively.

If the teacher is aware of how personal feelings are interfering in the interaction with a student, it may be useful to bring it up in some way, as I did with my patient in the matter of the madras jacket. So doing will indicate to the student that feelings are important in the interaction between the two of you and also that you are doing your best to focus on the student's feelings and not your own. Moreover, there is an implicit honesty in admitting that something personal may be distracting you from listening appropriately to the student. Such an admission reinforces the counseling relationship, even as it demonstrates your desire to pay as close attention to the student as you possibly can.

The Value of Silence

One important aspect of counseling on the run is the use of silence, also discussed in Chapter 1. In brief encounters where the teacher feels a demand for a response, the temptation is to talk, to find out, to "fix." But silence, properly used, is a very effective response, because it focuses attention on the student rather than on the teacher. Properly used, it puts the teacher in the facilitating position of being expectant. Consider the following example of how this can work.

Sally is a senior in a boarding school, and you are one of her dorm parents. She is a likeable but rather quiet person who does good academic work and is an unofficial student leader in the dorm. You notice that she seems quieter than usual after she returns from Christmas vacation—even rather distracted. She is clearly not herself. Her roommate mentioned to you yesterday that she is worried about Sally and thinks that there is something wrong at home. You find her alone after dinner, looking glum, invite her in for coffee and express your concern. She admits that she has been feeling down and has a lot on her mind. She then goes on to say that she thinks her mother is an alcoholic and that she does not know what to do, especially as her 12-year-old sister is still at home.

You might respond by saying that you can understand why she is upset; after a pause you say, "Tell me more." Now it is time to be quiet. Sally may have difficulty in talking, partly because she does not understand all of her emotions and her thoughts are jumbled up inside, partly because she feels some shame and social disapproval. The silence from you, if it is expectant, can be reassuring to Sally— perhaps more reassuring than if you were talking. She knows that you are giving her time to sort it out as she talks, and that in itself is a kind of caring or concern. To sit in the presence of another person who cares and does not push you can be comforting indeed. If the silence seems especially long at some point, you might offer the comment, "It must be hard to talk about" or "There must be a lot of different things going round and round in your head."

In this situation it will be helpful to remember that Sally has a problem only she can solve and that the problem is compounded of the facts of the situation at home and the mixture of feelings Sally has about those facts. In order to come to any solution she has to sort it all out; you cannot sort it out for her. The very best you can do is to provide an atmosphere in which that sorting out can get started. If you can keep this in mind, it is easier to be silent. Also, you will need to remember that silence does not indicate lack of interest, a fear that is often expressed by beginning counselors. As it turns out, quite the opposite is usually the case.

Silence is most effective if the teacher has first responded to the feelings, because it is an indication to the student that the two of you are on the same wavelength. With Sally, this took place in the comment that you could understand why she had been upset. Having established the common ground of feelings, silence can be meaningful as an opportunity to extend that common ground.

You may not need to spend a lot of time with Sally; indeed, you may not be able to do so because of your schedule or hers. You will, however, want to leave her with some clarifying comments about her feelings and to make an offer to pick up the conversation again soon. If she has talked about a variety of feelings, you might comment that she seems angry and scared and ashamed and loving toward her mother—all at the same time. You can understand why she feels perplexed and distracted, and does not know what to do. It may be difficult for you to let her go at this point with the situation unresolved, and you may wonder if Sally will want to talk further if you have not proposed a solution to her problem. Perhaps it seems paradoxical, but Sally is more likely to return if you have supported her struggle with the problem rather than taking it away from her by offering a solution. Silence is likely to be important in supporting that struggle.

In other words, one must keep the door open for subsequent contacts with the student—a goal of most, if not all, counseling-on-the-run interactions. As part of that process, it will be useful for the teacher to have in mind things to find out in future interactions with the student, especially questions about feelings and the connections between feelings and events. The questions and answers do not need to come all at once, and some will never have to be asked or answered, but it is an important counseling task to keep them at work in the teacher's mind. The teacher may wonder with Sally how she feels about her mother when she is sober, how long the mother has had a drinking problem, how helpless Sally feels, and how "up front" she can be with her mother. With Janice the questions may concern her sense of self-esteem, her anxiety about being in control of her impulses, the extent and accuracy of her knowledge about homosexuality and her feelings about it, as well as her previous experience with close relationships. With Gerald the teacher may want to think about how he gets along with his father and other authority figures, what things make him angry and how he expresses his anger in different situations, and the extent to which he wants other people to solve his problems.

To reiterate, having the questions in mind is important, but that is not to say that they always have to be asked. The desirability of asking each question can be evaluated in future interactions, based in large part on how the student is working out the problem. Having the questions in mind, however, will keep the teacher focused on the student in subtle ways that will be conveyed in their various interactions. A questioning approach also aids the teacher in concentrating on the feeling aspects of the student's problem.

Even in brief encounters the teacher should assess the seriousness of the situation; Are there red flags that need careful attention at the moment? Can the student tolerate the discomfort? If it is likely that there will be some behavior problems, will they be unduly damaging to the student or the school? In a five-minute spar, no one can make good assessments all the time; we have to live with that limitation. One must remember that there are other people in the school who know the student and that there will be other occasions to see the student. We do our best, thinking of what we know about the student from the past and how he or she has handled being upset. We think of what we know about human behavior and try to assess how much the particular student's actions seem to be out of line—if at all. It is rare that we have real cause to worry, and most assessments relate to how soon we need to see the student again and what kinds of responses need to be made to facilitate good counseling in the next meeting.

The Confrontational Encounter

Thus far, the description of counseling on the run has centered on situations where the student has either come to the teacher directly (as with Gerald) or responded to the teacher's questions or interest by describing and identifying a problem (as with Janice and Sally). There are other times when a more confrontational stance may be involved, when the teacher seeks out a student who may be reluctant to talk about a known or suspected problem, or when the teacher has a disciplinary role. How can counseling-on-the-run techniques be used on those occasions?

Consider another scenario. Jill is a junior in a day school. You teach French, are the assistant lacrosse coach, and are her adviser. Jill has missed some lacrosse practice sessions and does not work very hard in those she attends. She expresses a dislike of school to her friends at practice. When you talk with her about her work in your French class, she declares emphatically that "school is boring." She has even told you that "school stinks," and when she thought she was out of your hearing, but wasn't, the expletive was stronger. You have also noticed that at the last two practices she had the smell of alcohol on her breath. Midterm grades have just been released, and Jill's grades have declined. You leave a note for her to come and see you, and she does so nearly half an hour late.

Clearly, as her adviser, you have a responsibility to talk with Jill about her grades, her dogging it in practice, and her "bad attitude." At the same time, her anger and rebelliousness suggest a struggle within her about her sense of self. She may be somewhat confused as to who she is, and underneath, she may have some depression. Her anger is maladaptive and probably will continue to be that way until some of the underlying emotional issues are addressed. Your assessment suggests that possibly long-term counseling would be in order, but you do not have time for that. As a matter of fact, you have only a short time right now to deal with Jill.

This type of counseling on the run is somewhat different in that the first task is to express your concern about Jill's aberrant behavior, beginning with her clearest departures from the norm: her lower grades and the practice sessions she has missed. You comment on her statements that she does not like school and finds it boring. You may or may not want to make reference to the smell of alcohol; at the moment that is not the central issue, and reference to it could well lead to denial by Jill and further confrontation between you.

Having expressed your concern, as briefly and succinctly as possible, it is time to be quiet and hear what Jill has to say. Doing so may be difficult, for there may be a strong impulse to admonish Jill and to get her in line. To an angry and troubled student, that course might appear judgmental and make it difficult for her to share any of her feelings. On the other hand, if you are quiet, Jill may not say much or may repeat that school is boring and that she does not care, or she may express some annoyance that you are on her case so much. Of these possible variations, the majority of teachers are probably most uneasy with the idea that Jill will not say anything. How do you end that silence? You might, for example, say that you can understand why she finds it difficult to talk to you but that you are still concerned. If she clings to the theme that school is boring, you can ask her to tell you more. If she tells you to get off her case, you can respond that you are aware of her anger but are nevertheless still concerned. In any of these possibilities there may be occasion for reflecting some of Jill's feelings. She probably will not offer much opportunity, but whatever response you give to the little that is forthcoming may produce more now or in a later session.

The teacher as adviser deals with the fact that Jill's grades have declined and her performance on the lacrosse field is not up to standard. The teacher as counselor is concerned with Jill's behavior and wants to hear more about it, being ready to respond to the facts of her feelings if there is an opportunity. The teacher's responses to Jill as adviser and as counselor are an example of the classic "two hats" role that teachers have to fill. Teachers often are reluctant to do counseling because of the belief that they cannot wear two hats, that as advisers they cannot also use counseling techniques, and that the two roles interfere with each other. On the contrary, one of the lessons we have learned from teachers is that a counseling approach can, in fact, often strengthen the advising role.

The teacher/adviser will probably need to make another contact with Jill quite soon to express concern once more. As a matter of fact, Jill's situation is an example of one in which counseling on the run may have an advantage over more traditional or conventional counseling procedures. Jill's shield against the world, especially the adult world, will not easily be turned aside in a single counseling session even of half an hour or fifty minutes. By underscoring the realities— the declining grades and poor performance on the lacrosse field— while, at the same time, expressing concern and an interest in developing a relationship that will allow Jill to talk about her anger and boredom, the teacher/adviser makes it possible for Jill to lower her defenses a bit. She may not be able to handle more than a few minutes of dealing with feelings or considering a relationship in the first encounter. In a second contact the teacher/adviser repeats the "message," with the hope that Jill will recognize that it is genuine. Again, there may be value in brevity, giving Jill her own space, not crowding her, yet helping her realize that there is an adult who wants to help. Still a third contact may be necessary before Jill is ready to respond with any expression of her deeper feelings.

Consistency of approach will be the key emphasis on the part of the teacher/adviser, sticking to the facts, not admonishing her unduly, and being expectant and interested in her feelings and how they impact her current life. Listening carefully, allowing silences, and resonating with feelings when they are evident demonstrate that consistency. It is possible, of course, that Jill may never open up, that her emotional problems will make it too difficult for her to do so. Any teacher, whether using the counseling approach or not, has to be prepared for that eventuality. But the brief interactions which characterize counseling on the run offer substantial likelihood that something constructive may happen for Jill.

A more explicit confrontation comes when a student has broken a rule and been caught at it. The teacher, dorm parent, or dean then has to act as a disciplinarian, facing the student with the infraction and setting a punishment, or putting in motion a process that will involve punishment. This role of the teacher is clear. Is there any place in it for a counseling approach? In our work with teachers we are clear that counseling should not replace discipline, that rules and structure are important in the developing life of the adolescent. Firmness and consistency in disciplinary matters are important ingredients, but there often can be an opportunity for counseling after the discipline has been dealt with. A teacher or dean can wear two hats as long as a clear distinction is made between the roles. Making that distinction allows the teacher to go beyond the infraction of a rule and its appropriate punishment and perhaps to help the student understand how his or her feelings, and conflicts about those feelings, are leading to maladaptive behavior. The experience, including the discipline, can be viewed as part of growing up or maturing. This is an ideal situation, of course, but short-term contacts, using some counseling-on-the-run techniques, may make a disciplinary situation a truly educational one.

Consider the case of Joel, a second-year sophomore in your dormitory. He has been an itch all fall, because he has pushed the limits a great deal. Your school has a rule that students are to be in their rooms each weekday evening between 7:30 and 9:30 for study and are not to disturb other students on the floor. They are not allowed to play music because the sound could bother students in adjoining rooms. One evening, Joel is playing music softly during the study period. A student across the hall asks him to turn it off. In response Joel verbally abuses him and goes into his room and dumps the contents of his wastebasket all over the floor. You are quite familiar with Joel's voice and clearly recognize it when the argument erupts. You go into the hall to get the facts, then tell Joel to come into your sitting room. In the back of your mind you recall that Joel is the younger brother of a very attractive senior girl in the school, an all-A student and president of her class as well as a ranking freestyle swimmer. Joel is short, only an average student, and—unlike his sister—seems to have missed his father's athletic genes. You can understand his frustration, but clearly he has broken an important rule in the dorm.

When you are face-to-face with Joel, away from the other students, you can tell him that he has broken an important rule. For this he must pay the consequences: going to supervised study in the large lecture hall, and for the next month not being able to leave school during the week to go into town. You also tell him that if he breaks these restrictions the matter will go to the dean of students for further action. Joel may argue about the deed or the punishment, but you remain firm and say, "That's the way it is."

Having worn your disciplinarian's hat, you might now exchange it for the counseling hat and ask Joel how things are going for him. He may want to pursue the rule infraction or punishment, in response to which you can say that the case is closed. He may say that you are picking on him, that the punishment is unfair, and that he does not get a fair shake at school. You might be tempted to say that is not true, or that he has created his own problems, all of which you feel to be accurate. Or you could ask him what it feels like to be picked on and not get a fair shake in things.

Very likely, the central feeling to contend with is Joel's anger, which he has been expressing all term in his stretching of the rules and his disagreements with other students. The force of that anger could well be turned on you. This is worthy of comment because most teachers, and professional therapists as well, do not like to deal with students, or patients, who are angry. In our work with teachers at the Institutes, the most common difficulties reported in counseling students are dealing with the angry student, or the one who refuses to talk. Disciplinary situations very frequently bring forth anger, sometimes expressed directly and forcefully, sometimes subdued and smoldering. Under these circumstances, teachers usually try to protect themselves, which is a rather natural and basic defense. It may not serve the student best, however, from a counseling point of view. Rather than engaging in a combative interaction, the teacher needs to acknowledge in some manner the student's anger and to provide an opportunity for its release. But teachers often feel that if they do this, students will perceive them as weak, that they will lose some of their power and superior status. This feeling could well be a reflection of their own unease, that they are weak if they do not fight back in some way. But the student will have difficulty in understanding his or her actions and in using the incident constructively without some acknowledgment by the teacher of the anger. By so doing the teacher also has the opportunity to begin, or contribute to, one of the most important aspects of any kind of counseling—namely, a relationship.

For example, Joel not only sounded very angry, but when he said that it was not fair and that you were always picking on him, his aggressive posture made his anger obvious. You can probably imagine a number of other angry things that he might have said. Joel's pressure needs some release. This could be accomplished by saying, "I can understand your being really ticked off and angry," and then letting Joel continue, being silent and giving him the opportunity to talk. Once again, the less said, the better, as long as what is said resonates with Joel's feeling state. Before the counseling-on-the-run interaction with Joel is finished, the teacher might connect this response with the anger noted earlier, wondering what it feels like to be picked on and not get a fair shake.

If the scenario with Joel had worked out this way, the teacher would have kept the two hats separate, dealing with the discipline first and maintaining consistency about that, then dealing with the counseling aspects as subsequent and separate issues. If the situation is handled correctly, the teacher will not lose authority or respect and is likely to set in motion a process for Joel that can be helpful to him.

Ongoing Counseling

Up to this point the focus of counseling on the run has been on a single situation, with the suggestion that in some cases follow-up interactions might profitably take place. As a matter of fact, there is a real opportunity for ongoing counseling interactions with a student, perhaps over the course of a whole academic year, using the techniques that have been outlined in this chapter. Usually when one thinks of counseling it is of the ongoing process characteristic of the therapist's office, a regular meeting of an hour or so once a week, or something of that sort. Understandably teachers may not find it easy to think of themselves as being able to counsel over the course of a year if they have this view of the process. Not only is the time commitment unrealistic and forbidding, but there may also be the sense that ongoing counseling involves sophisticated techniques beyond those possessed by the teacher. This is often expressed as the fear of "getting in over one's head." Based on what we have learned from teachers at North-field and Fountain Valley, our thesis is that counseling on the run can be intermittent as to the occurrence of the interactions, variable as to the length of time any interaction lasts, and simple and direct in terms of the techniques used. On this basis it is easily managed over a school year, or even longer. The one new element above and beyond the procedures mentioned thus far is that of a relationship.

Almost always a central factor in the success of psychotherapy or counseling of any kind is the quality of the relationship between the two parties. This is a special type of relationship, and it has certain features which are particularly important, as noted elsewhere both in this chapter and in Chapter 1. What follows, then, is a summary or reiteration.

For one person to work on emotional problem solving in collaboration with another person, no matter how regular and intense or irregular and moderate, there must be trust and a sense of safe space. The student needs to know that what he or she has to say will be accepted, at least initially, without judgment or admonishment. Once a relationship has been established there may well be a place for the teacher to express an opinion about a student's behavior or actions, but even then it will need to be presented in the context of information for the student to use in problem solving. Safe space, then, means a place where the student can talk about powerful—perhaps frightening—feelings, can share unease, and can reveal vulnerability—and not have to suffer for it. For students, a sense of safe space will not come about because the teacher declares it but through the kinds of responses the teacher makes, especially those which resonate with the student's feelings, and through the silences, the "sitting with the student" while he or she tries to sort things out.

Trust will be enhanced if the teacher cares about the student and is concerned about that person's internal struggles. We sometimes equate caring and concern with affection or loving. The feelings often do go together, but as noted in Chapter 1, a teacher who is competent in counseling will keep some distance in the relationship and not let the affection felt for the student interfere with the student's problem solving. The danger of getting too close occurs when the student does things or says things to make the teacher feel good rather than dealing realistically with the problem. This does not mean that the teacher has to suspend liking a student or feeling warm and affectionate about him or her; rather the teacher must monitor and control those feelings. A phrase from medical and psychotherapeutic practice is relevant here: "detached concern," some aspect of which can enhance the activity of the teacher as counselor. Then, a student can feel the caring and concern but not be burdened by it.

Another facet of trust comes about through the teacher's control of the tendency toward gratification of his or her own needs. For example, the teacher makes sure that the relationship with the student does not fulfill a need by the teacher to exert control or be dominant, to exact retribution, to put the student down, to experience sexual excitement or titillation, or to feel morally smug. By controlling the fulfillment of these needs, the teacher does not exploit the student and does not use the student's pain and struggle for his or her own gain. The student will probably not be conscious of this control by the teacher, but there will be more trust because there is no exploitation.

In the consulting room we know about the importance of confidentiality; from teachers we have learned its value in working with students. We have also learned from teachers how tempted they are to talk about students and their problems, often under the guise of wanting to do everything they can to help a student. We know that teachers often struggle with this temptation, finding it difficult to resist the pleasure of gossip. At the same time, however, they are aware of the meaning to a student of a teacher who can keep his or her mouth shut. Trust and safe space are enhanced by clarity about confidentiality.

The final point is a subtle one: Trust is built as the teacher conveys the belief that the student has the capacity to solve his or her own problems and that the teacher is a guide or facilitator in that process. In my work as a therapist I often think of my task as speaking or responding to the health of my patients. This attitude, once again, puts the focus on the student, not the teacher, and has great power in mobilizing forces within the student. It is a kind of trust which the teacher has in the student, and it thereby enhances the trust in the relationship.

Testing the Limits

When a teacher has an ongoing counseling relationship with a student, one thing that will almost always occur—often more than once—is what we call "testing." Often the student will not be aware of doing so. Initially the purpose of the testing will be to discover if there is trust in the relationship. Later it will be a reflection of some of the underlying issues in adolescent development or particular problems in the student's life. Testing is very prevalent in intensive counseling where there are weekly sessions of some length, but the teacher who does counseling on the run should be prepared for it as well. Some examples will be useful in understanding this aspect of the counseling interaction.

A student may become angry with the teacher for little or no apparent reason or show an exaggerated degree of anger. Of the students cited in this chapter, Gerald and Jill were angry to begin with and they expressed their anger in an overt manner. Such anger might continue, in part, to find out whether the teacher can deal with it and whether the teacher will become punitive, as both these students might expect from past experiences. The same might be said for Joel. The teacher may be perplexed when Sally says in subsequent sessions that she is wasting her time talking about the problem and that the teacher really does not understand—all said with a glower and a stare of sullen annoyance. If the teacher has felt Sally's pain, felt real empathy, he or she will likely be taken aback by the anger.

A second type of testing is in avoidance or distancing, either in directly avoiding the teacher by not coming to see him or her, sitting at a distance from the teacher in the dining room, or talking very little when they do get together. This conduct can be puzzling if the student previously has been quite open and apparently grateful for the teacher's attention. Distancing can be caused by the student's experiencing disturbing strong emotions which actually come from the work or problem solving which he or she is doing, making some connections between events, experiences, and feelings. In this case the distancing comes from trying to reduce the intensity of the feelings—to withdraw while working at figuring things out. The distancing can also be caused by the student's uneasiness about the closeness perceived in the developing relationship with the teacher. Jill, for example, could be both pleased and frightened by the fact that an important adult cared about her and tried to understand her.

Testing can take place when the student apparently becomes dependent on the teacher, hanging around places in the school where the teacher is likely to be or coming by the office or dorm room every day. Either overtly or covertly the student may push the teacher to be more helpful in solving the problem, asking that the teacher take his or her side in dealing with the school or parents. Basically, the student is asking to be taken care of. Many teachers feel quite uneasy with such dependence, are fearful that it may happen, and do not know what to do with it when it does happen. There may be two aspects to the testing: to find out if the teacher really cares and genuinely likes the student, and, more unconsciously, to find out how the teacher will set limits and still care for the student. Of all the kinds of testing, this one can be the most frustrating and may lead the teacher to do some distancing unless he or she can see the dependence for what it is and eventually help the student understand this behavior.

Finally, the student may talk about fairly drastic behavior as contemplated action—for example, leaving the school either to attend another school or to return home; running away; doing drugs or drinking a lot. Such actions are phrased in the context of, "What the hell, I don't care!" and there may be talk about suicide or wondering if life is worth living. Again, the function of the testing is to find out whether the teacher really cares, whether he or she can take it, how strong he or she is, and how much he or she can be relied on. We can think of such talk as trying to get the teacher's attention—which it usually does, and quite quickly. Most teachers find their anxiety rising in such circumstances, sometimes to an uncomfortable degree. The facilitative aspect of such anxiety is to alert the teacher to the possibility that testing in the relationship can be one aspect of the student's motivation for talking about drastic behavior.

In dealing with testing behavior, one of the most important responses on the teacher's part is constancy: focusing on the student's feelings, keeping extraneous material out of the interaction, and keeping the problem-solving activity of the student at the center. The teacher must adapt to each student—that is, concentrate on the important areas for that person: Gerald's frustration with authority figures, Janice's confusion about sexuality and friendship, Sally's love, anger, and helplessness regarding her mother, Jill's tough exterior and inner wish to be liked, and Joel's worries about being accepted and having to prove himself. I like to think of this process as keeping the threads of the discourse clear over time in a constant way to help the student stay with the important emotional issues.

After the teacher becomes aware that testing might be taking place, he or she can begin to wonder with the student about what might be happening in their relationship. I use the word "wonder" to indicate a curiosity that both teacher and student might have—an exploring attitude rather than a pronouncement by the teacher about what is happening. A pronouncement is more like an interpretation, as discussed and warned about in Chapter 1. A pronouncement by the teacher also shifts the focus away from the student and his or her problem-solving ability. Wondering or questioning together keeps the student working on the problem, trying to figure it out.

To the student who responds with exaggerated anger, the teacher might say, "Your anger is really boiling—that I hear—but I'm also a little puzzled, wondering if the intensity of it might have something to do with what is going on between us." To the student who is avoiding the teacher an appropriate comment might be, "I haven't seen you lately. I don't want to intrude, but I wondered how you felt after the last time we talked, and how you felt about me afterward?" To the dependent student the response could take a number of directions, one of which is, "You seem to be depending on me a lot lately, and I sense that this is becoming pretty important to you. What do you think could be going on with you?" To the student who talks about drastic behavior, one might say, "That sounds pretty serious. I'm concerned, but I also wonder what you might want from me and how you feel about our relationship?" Once again, it will be important not to say too much, to let a question hang in the air, and not to phrase the wondering or questioning in any kind of judgmental, punitive, or rejecting manner.

At times, in dealing with testing behavior, it may be helpful to the student to have the teacher set limits. These may relate to the amount of time a teacher has available or the kinds of things a teacher can hear without bringing in other members of the school administration. They may also relate to limitations on rule breaking and on understanding of what kinds of behavior the teacher has to report, as well as parameters on the expression of certain emotions—abusive anger, for example. A student who is struggling and upset is often grateful to know that an adult can set limits which the student is unable to impose himself or herself. The relationship between teacher and student can be enhanced if the limit setting by the teacher is done with both caring and constancy. Beginning counselors are often uneasy about setting limits, afraid that in so doing they will impair the working relationship. With experience, they realize that careful limit setting will enhance the relationship over the long run.

Conclusion

In conclusion, it is important to pick up once again the comparison of therapy in the consulting room and counseling on the run. We have noted that these activities differ in time involved, privacy available, and opportunity for two people to work together in an intense and intimate manner. We also have noted that, despite the differences, there are many common elements and the basic tenents of work in the consulting room apply to counseling on the run. What we have not done thus far is to speak of the advantages of the latter for a school situation, the special value that counseling on the run can have for a school and for its students.

By the nature of the low student-to-faculty ratio, the close inter-action between faculty and students, and the emphasis placed by independent schools on individual attention, there is ample opportunity for a teacher to keep in touch with a student. This situation exists in either day or boarding school, and "keeping in touch" can be done on an informal basis. A teacher can follow up on a conversation by a few words after class in the parking lot or over the lunch table, keeping the thread of the previous interaction, touching on the feelings that were present, and letting the student know that his or her concern is still there. The therapist in the consulting room cannot do that. For the teacher, these informal continuations of an initial interaction do much to enhance the counseling relationship, and at the same time they give the student his or her own space to work on the problem. Also, there is a naturalness to keeping in touch that keeps the counseling on the run from being "shrinky" and that subtly emphasizes the health of the student and his or her capacity to work out problems independently. There is a great deal of power in these informal contacts that teachers may not realize—power that can further counseling.

Closely allied is the power inherent in the teacher's concern for the student, which may be undervalued by most teachers. To have an adult want to know—*really* want to know—what the student is feeling, not to crowd the student in sorting things out, and not to try to tell him or her what to do may be a new and unusual experience for many adolescents. The effect on the student may not be immediate in terms of change in behavior, and the student may not be able to convey a reaction to the teacher, but the long-term effects can be substantial. Thus, there is little likelihood that there will be any immediate reward for the teacher; satisfaction will have to be internal.

In the course of this chapter, there has been more and more emphasis on the relationship in counseling on the run. This concept is central to sorting through the emotional issues and conflicts the student is struggling with. A school has always been an important place for such relationships to develop, in part because teacher and student have a common interest apart from counseling—that of education. They are joined in learning, in discovery, in thinking, in the excitement of intellectual challenge and growth. To be sure, some of learning is boring and hard and even pedestrian, but the common task that the student and teacher share is like a matrix, something that is larger than each of them but something in which they both share. All of this can strengthen the relationship between them and give it a special quality that therapists in the consulting room never, or rarely, have. With the context of education in which the counseling relationship takes place, it can be nurtured in infrequent, brief contacts and in the most public of places, as well as in those moments when the teacher and student have time together by themselves.

This chapter began and has focused on students with problems; indeed the whole book is in that vein. It is perhaps appropriate to conclude by emphasizing the theme that emerged near the end of the chapter: that counseling on the run can mobilize health and adaptive capacity within the student. The great majority of students have the capacity to cope in varying degrees. They may not have been given sufficient credit for it or may not have been allowed to practice it much, and they may be frightened of the mistakes they have made when they tried to cope. But the capacity is there, waiting to be touched and energized by the teacher. Furthermore, the tradition of education as we know it in Western societies implicitly assumes a basic reservoir of ability to deal with the world. One of the most exciting things that an adolescent can experience in growing up is an interaction with a valued adult who has implicit faith in the capacity of that student to sort things through successfully. No finer gift can any teacher give a student.

Chapter 3

ADOLESCENCE: DEVELOPMENTAL STAGE AND EVOLUTIONARY PROCESS

Paul A. Walters, Jr.

Adolescence is an "olympic torch" time of life—that time when, ideally, the best of one generation is passed on to the next. For most adolescents, this passage is not accomplished in a stadium to the cheers of multitudes, but more quietly and inexorably in the home and in the school. The influence of culture on adolescence has been the basis of many writings. Some of these, such as those by Erikson, have been quite specific, others have been less so. Most have not emphasized sufficiently the fact that parents and teachers in almost equal measure provide the most important sources of external guidance in a young person's life. From the outset, any discussion of adolescence has to acknowledge that fact.

Not at the expense, however, of two important internal factors: biologic development, which is heralded by puberty, physical growth, and cognitive development, and psychosocial maturation, which is manifested by consolidation of the inner self and by the growing complexities of attachments. The process and outcome of adolescence, therefore, is inextricably linked to the interplay between these four influences: two external, parents and school; two internal, the formation of the biological and psychological self and the establishment of the capacity for friends and lovers.

45

More importantly, these external and internal factors are not static. On the contrary, they are under constant evolution as the demands of social class, gender, allowed behaviors, and encouraged aspirations shift from generation to generation. Because of these shifts, students of adolescent development have to constantly ask themselves, "What constitutes adolescence today? Is what is identified now by adults as behavior typical of adolescence experienced as such by most young people?" Students in classes about adolescent development have pointed out repeatedly that such is not the case. To understand adolescence today, then, it is necessary to understand changes that have occurred in the family and the schools and how these changes have affected the internal factors of biologic and psychological maturation and attachment.

An Historical Perspective

Furnishing valuable historical perspective, Kett[1] made the observation that, in any period, those who have written about youth have worn blinders. These blinders allow them to discern only those young people whose experiences fit these writers' notions about characteristic behavior in adolescence. Taking this point further, there is a marked difference between an adolescent youth of today—as typified by the alienated students in the popular movie of the middle eighties, "The Breakfast Club"—and an adolescent of the pioneer period of the early 1800s, a factory worker of the 1870s, or a Boy Scout of the 1920s. Theories formulated during these different periods have said as much about the period or about the observer of the period as about the young people being observed.

For example, in the 1960s what Kenniston[2] first characterized as postmodern youth is a group of young people with varying degrees of psychological maturity who are unwilling to become involved in conventional occupational and family life. Alienation from the culture and ambivalence about conventional ties seem to form core attitudes for these young people. These attitudes still persist among a segment of young people, but in no way do they typify or represent a modal

[1]Joseph F. Kett, *Rites of Passage* (New York: Basic Books, 1977), pp. 3–7.
[2]Kenneth Kenniston, "Youth: A 'New' Stage of Life," *The American Scholar* 39 (Autumn 1970), pp. 361–641.

value among adolescents of the eighties. Rather, they say more about Kenniston, the sixties, and ambivalence about adulthood characteristic of that period.

Today, adults are as likely to be ambivalent about adolescence as adolescents are about adulthood. Adults look back on their own adolescence with varying degrees of bemusement, envy, nostalgia and regret, and they project these feelings on those they are observing. Today's adolescents, on the other hand, are neither world-weary, alienated from convention, nor mistrustful of adults. Like any segment of American society, they are an incredibly diverse group of people who live their lives in ways that are quite unlike popular stereotypes.

In fact, it is this stereotyping that has blinded adults to the acknowledgment that adolescents of today are as diverse a group of young people as they are. Before adults allow themselves to be swayed into thinking that the young people portrayed on television, in movies, in magazines, or in the nightly news represent typical teenagers, it would be wise to remember that the adolescents portrayed in the information and entertainment media are consumers. Adolescent culture, whatever else it is, is a very important consumer segment of the American population. For example, in ads adolescents are portrayed as slim, attractive, and active—ideals accepted by the majority of young people. In reality, however, the average weight of most people has increased, many young people don't exercise, and many fewer than those in advertisements feel themselves to be attractive. This ideal has arisen from a stereotype created by a consumer-oriented segment of adult society which emphasizes the attainment of a physical ideal as it relates to market strategy.

For large segments of the adult community, therefore, adolescence is a time in which behavior is driven by the development of a lifestyle marked by consumerism and by achievement in school and on standardized tests. In fact, prosperity and success for some young people arrive in the teens, giving rise to the idea that prosperity and success are fickle rather than hard-won. If they are neither middle class nor superior achievers on standardized testing, success is an elusive goal beyond their reach. Broadly speaking, then, adolescent behavior is driven by two quests: prosperity as measured by consumerism and achievement as measured by testing.

In a more classical vein, adolescence is also a time in which behavior is determined to a large extent by the formation of ideals. Here, fortunately, development is not mortgaged to broader cultural interests. This aspect of growth resides firmly in the home with the parents. Daniel Offer, in several longitudinal studies, has clearly demonstrated that most young people obtain both their values and their aspirations from parental guidance, example, and encouragement. In summary, adolescent group behavior may appear to be driven by cultural forces, but for individuals behavior is also led by the formation of ideals shaped within the family.

The Influence of the School

The school must be responsive to the influences of both the larger culture and of the family. Some theorists have seen adolescence as a stage of life which evolved out of the industrial revolution. But this is only a partial truth. It would be more accurate to say that, as technology has become more and more complex, a prolonged educational apprenticeship has become essential. Acceptance of this necessity is so widespread in our present culture that the British sociologist, Musgrove[3], was led to observe that the good American home is one which is cooperative with the educational system. It follows, then, that the "bad" home is one which allows truancy from school or disruptive behavior within school.

Classically, adolescent development is intertwined with educational progress and achievement. Traits that have been emphasized relate to the inculcation of autonomy, the acquisition of skills, and the establishment of competence in one or more areas. Examined more closely, however, the developmental focus of these traits is educational, and failure to acquire these competencies is considered deviant or even illustrative of mental illness. The school system, therefore, is in collusion with both the home and the culture to define adolescence in a manner congruent with higher education.

In the last century a high school diploma was necessary to resolve two issues. It furnished a passport from the farm, and it prevented early entry into the unskilled labor pool. Today a college diploma is necessary for the same purposes—namely, entrance into the skilled work force, which for most is postponed until the early or middle twenties.

---

[3]Frank Musgrove, *The Family, Education, and Society* (New York: Rutledge & Kegan Paul, Ltd., 1966), pp. 72–93.

Early Adulthood

For various reasons some young people are not able to proceed into higher education. For them adulthood begins earlier and is marked by entry into the workforce or into parenthood after high school. These young people, forced into early adulthood, face additional dilemmas not confronted by the more fortunate peers who are able to remain within the educational system. Namely, their work opportunities are limited and an expanded work role or career is doubtful. In addition, for those unfortunate few who are teen parents, there are other obstacles. First of all, affordable cultural supports outside the immediate family are practically nonexistent. For those who are alienated from their families or those whose families are not able to furnish child care, a work career is severely compromised or, for many, nonexistent. These latter young women find themselves locked into unemployment despite their wishes to find work. With the road to higher education blocked by an early entry into adulthood, these young people are likely to feel a sense of failure, alienation, or futility unless they are the minority who have a family or community that supports them in breaking away from this route.

For this segment of youth whose adolescence has been terminated prematurely, the development of skills which emphasize continuity of attachments, family, social networking, and interest in helping people is necessary to insure their entry into service industries rather than technological ones. If this is not done, opportunities for these young people will be more severely constrained than those of their more affluent, educationally adept, and traditionally success-oriented counterparts.

This two-tiered division of youth is divided into those whose adolescence is curtailed prematurely by early entry into adulthood and those who are able to prolong the teen years. The early adult segment of this population contains a disproportionate number of young people from single-parent homes headed by women as well as from minority homes. Several observations are worthy of attention in this regard. The first is that one of three teenagers in this country by 1990 will be a minority. The second is that minorities from intact middle class homes are doing exceptionally well, better than their white counterparts in some states. Another is that minorities from single-parent homes headed by women are doing very, very badly. Young women from this group have the highest teenage birth rate, and the young men have a high incidence of delinquency, crime, violence, and early death. Many of the studies on adolescence have not included this segment of the population in developmental schema, but these people are casualties of the system which makes prolonged youth, as defined by affluence and higher education, mandatory.

Prolonged Adolescence

Their more affluent counterparts may be more fortunate because of more numerous options, but this path of development has its dilemmas also. First of all, the high school classroom prior to the 1950s was likely to be representative of the community, in which degrees of aptitude were blended together. The diversity of the community was preserved intact and a young person's peers and friends were likely to represent various degrees of aptitude, career aspirations, and levels of achievement. The atmosphere was more cooperative and the stresses were largely social.

After World War II, however, young people with similar levels of achievement and aspiration as measured by both grades and by standardized testing were placed in similar "tracks." Peers had similar goals and potential rather than similar backgrounds or neighborhoods. Young people, therefore, were brought together in the classroom because of similar talents rather than shared interests, backgrounds, or friends. As a result the peer culture became more immediately and consistently competitive. For both privileged and disadvantaged alike, stress became an inescapable part of high achievement. In this atmosphere of competitive stress, the challenge of learning became subjugated to achievement and rivalry superseded collaboration. This emphasis on competition and rivalry at the expense of cooperation and collaboration has led to relative social alienation and isolation and has interfered with the ultimate development of an educational community.

Secondly, adolescence as a developmental stage has been prolonged by the near necessity of higher education. Adolescents are thus placed in a paradoxical situation. On the one hand, better nutrition and general health have resulted in physical maturity at an earlier age than previous generations; on the other hand, the attainment of adult status as measured by financial independence, a career, and a family has been pushed by prolonged schooling further into the future with each generation.

The Blurred Line Between Adolescence and Adulthood

At the same time adolescents have been allowed more and more adult prerogatives without having to take the ultimate responsibility for their actions. For example, teenagers make the same decisions about relationships, use of substances, sexual activity, management of financial resources, and childbearing as their adult counterparts. Thus, while adolescence as a stage of development has been prolonged, life as lived by this age group is virtually indistinguishable from that of young adults. Adolescents, therefore, have many of the advantages and problems of adults but little of the ultimate responsibility for their actions—an enviable position which most young people want to maintain.

For their part, many adults see young people as privileged, irresponsible, lazy, alienated, rebellious, ungrateful—the list of pejoratives continues indefinitely. In contrast, however, there is little evidence which suggests that the values, aspirations, and long-term goals of adolescents are substantively different from those of adults. Their behavior may appear less responsible to the adult, but it reflects a sense of freedom among teenagers. These prerogatives and privileges, free from final commitment, have aroused envy among adults.

This envy is shown in various ways. One is by stereotyping youth with pejoratives which have changed little through the generations since antiquity. Another stereotype is the attribution of countercultural aspects of adolescent behavior as representative of the majority rather than as the actions of relatively few—as occurred in the sixties. During that time both radicals and hippies, widely dissimilar groups, were thought to represent the new generation of young people; in actuality, they portrayed less than an estimated 10 percent of their age cohorts. Still another stereotypic concept of adolescents is that, inevitably, they will be afflicted by anxiety, depression, and other symptoms of turmoil and crisis which require professional evaluation. Periods of stress accompanied by some turmoil accompany any major life change, and most do not need professional intervention. In fact, there is no evidence which definitively proves that the incidence of mental illness is greater among an adolescent cohort than among a comparable adult group.

These manifestations of stereotypic thinking and adult ambivalence create in young people a sense of alienation from the adult community. For most adolescents this alienation is tempered by peer relationships, which provide reassurance, sustenance, and impetus for further growth. For some, this peer culture is recreational; for others, it is central and becomes arrayed against the values of the culture. However, for those whose development is continuous, evolutionary, and normative rather than tumultuous or deviant, the family remains central as the ultimate refuge and source of affirmation and encouragement.

Roles of Parents and Schools

The role of parents is to encourage and affirm the aspirations and ideals of their children through the continuity and nurturance of their relationship throughout adolescence. This continuity of love and affirmation is equal in importance to the more traditional developmental issues of autonomy and competence. The adolescent, therefore, is confronted by tension between the ties of old relationships within the family and the encroachment of adult demands in which autonomy from these ties is considered necessary for optimal growth. The reaction of the young person to even benign parental interest under these circumstances varies from that of resentful dependence to laconic forebearance. For their part, parents during this time of conflicting pulls must remain steadfast in love and respect, available for counsel, and encouraging about the future, thus making it possible for young people to preserve the integrity of the relationship, even under protest.

For many parents, however, availability is a central issue. For example, at the present time only 7 percent of intact homes contain one wage earner; in the rest, both parents hold jobs. In these families time as much as money becomes a crucial issue. While child care is not as crucial a day-to-day activity for adolescent children as for those in primary school, some time must be made available for them. Parents need to be available to prevent unacceptable behavior from becoming habitual. In contrast to primary school children for whom day care is available for those with financial resources, child care for adolescent children is largely unavailable in the marketplace and unacceptable to the teen. Not only is the aphorism, "The bigger the child, the larger the problem" true, but community facilities for nonproblem teenagers are woefully limited.

More often than not, the school becomes the defacto day care facility for the teenage child in families in which both parents or a single parent work. Public schools are largely inadequate for this role unless the youngster is an athlete, artistically gifted, or a school leader. For those parents who have the financial resources or gifted children, the private school which offers a broad range of after-hours activities for their students may fulfill this role. The remaining majority of young people, however, are left to the limited resources of the community or to each other. This is particularly true for the young people of single parents.

Single-parent families, the most rapidly increasing family segment, comprise mostly single women. To compound their difficulties, these women have half the financial resources of their male counterparts. In addition, if they are of a racial or ethnic minority, these mothers are very likely to have inadequate resources to cope with both the demands of a job and the developmental needs of their adolescent children. With insufficient time for parenting and inadequate financial resources for alternative care, the single mother often watches helplessly as her teenage children become mired in maladaptive forms of adolescent passage such as substance abuse, truancy, delinquency, gang membership, petty theft, and even felonious activities. For the more fortunate children of single mothers, relatively speaking, early marriage and entry into the workforce might be the solution. For many of these young people, however, the progress to better things has been blocked by premature closure of adolescence either through antisocial activities or through early adoption of an adult role.

Successful negotiation of adolescence, then, is dependent on an intact home, preferably with adequate financial resources, the ability to keep adolescent development in process by continuing education beyond secondary school, and the maintenance of ties with those adults who are most caring—parents and, often, teachers. Adolescence, however, is equally influenced by internal change which, in the final analysis, represents the true evolution of adolescence. Puberty is the external manifestation of internal physiological changes which herald the beginning of this process. Moreover, there are internal psychological changes in cognition, self-esteem, self-image, and the capacity for attachment which are also crucial, and will be considered subsequently.

Development of Cognitive Competency

All of the above mentioned changes introduce the process of adolescence which may vary from a few years in more agrarian Western cultures to well over a decade in a modern technological society such as exists in the United States. As stated before, the complexities of our culture demand an extended apprenticeship, in the course of which prolonged education is the most successful means of maturation.

A major task of adolescence, therefore, involves the development of cognitive skills, Kagan[4] observed that the intellectual complexities of technology have evoked in man an innate cognitive potential which enables humans to solve complex intellectual tasks in a rational manner. This potential includes a preference for orderly serial thinking, the capacity to consider opposites as not mutually exclusive, the choice to use thought as an end in itself instead of solely as a preparation for action, and, finally, the ability to think about thinking, both of the self and of others. The establishment of these complex means of rational thinking among the majority of young people is in response to the complexities of modern technology, and, in turn, is responsible for further advances in this technology. The hierarchical pinnacle of cognitive evolution, then, is the ability to solve complex problems rationally, and educational progress is linked to this ability.

This evolutionary cognitive hierarchy has modified development in other ways also. First of all, the ability to solve complex cognitive tasks allows young people a considerable degree of autonomy. For many years this autonomy has included making one's own decisions whenever possible, examining the relevance of educational, political, and religious assumptions, and developing views as a unique individual about the meaning of life. Such intellectual autonomy resulted in the early formation of a philosophy of life which is meant to be unique to each individual and different in some ways from one's parents'. For

---

[4]Jerome Kagan, "A Conception of Early Adolescence," *Daedalus* (Fall 1971), pp. 997–1012.

example, ten years ago the formation of a meaningful philosophy of life together with becoming an authority in one's chosen field were the most important issues to students entering highly competitive institutions of higher learning. By 1983 being an authority in one's chosen field and being well off financially had eclipsed these. Despite their seeming difference, each set of these priorities represents not only an autonomous position arrived at through the use of rational cognitive skills but also continued emphasis on these skills in development. Furthermore, each of these priorities maintains a traditional goal: the development of the individual as an autonomous leader.

Secondly, this cognitive maturity allows adolescents to consider both the real and the possible. Earlier in development, children accept reality as that which is considered important by adults, and, for the most part, they adjust their behavior accordingly. Adolescents, as a part of the process of developing new cognitive competencies, question this reality as defined by adults and by schools. In doing this, they form their own definitions of a reality by which they attempt to live. This definition may be consonant or congruent with the expectations of adolescent behavior as defined by the culture, in which case it is considered traditional and development may be considered continuous. In contrast, some adolescents strenuously object to certain expectations and resist conforming. Their behavior could be described as variant: at some times conforming to expectations, at other times, not. But under these circumstances, development may still be continuous. To differentiate further, behavior of some adolescents may be clearly in opposition to the expectations of adults, in which case the behavior is deviant and development at this point may be thought of as tumultuous. Contrary to much popular writing and thinking, most adolescent behavior falls within the continuous range, maturity occurs by slow march rather than by dramatic vicissitudes, and developmental expectations are congruent with the goals of the culture.

Definitions of reality also involve serious consideration of what is real in terms of the exigencies of everyday life and what is possible in terms of the future. Adolescent development is always finely balanced between the real and the possible and the present and the future. The approximation of the real and possible vary from generation to generation. In the sixties, for example, the prevailing style among traditional youth was to keep all options open; the possibilities were unlimited. From this point of view, if one chose prematurely, opportunities might be lost. The present, then, was conditional and the future was concerned with that which might be possible. This was a more optimistic stance, in which experimentation was encouraged. In contrast, youth of the eighties are more attuned to the real, being concerned with definite careers rather than open possibilities. Katchadourian[5], somewhat whimsically, has alluded to the rise of careerism among today's youth as "going to the bank rather than to pot." This translates into the view that the purpose of higher education today is more utilitarian than that of enhancing options.

These two somewhat contradictory attitudes indicate that the use of cognitive competency to order priorities depends as much on cultural emphases as on intrapersonal gifts. In some generations the consideration of open-ended possibilities is of the highest priority; in others the early acceptance of definite career tracks is more encouraged. In this vein, Katchadourian further observed that the stance an adolescent takes about the future is more dependent on parental guidance than on institutional encouragement. Thus, concern about the future among adults may add another pressure to make an early career choice during adolescence. Furthermore, this concern with the definite rather than open-ended possibilities leaves the youth of today, as observed by Offer[6], in a slightly less optimistic stance than those of the sixties. Thus, the use to which a young person puts his developing cognitive competence is influenced by the attitude of parents as much as schools, which, in turn, determine his attitude toward future education.

Finally, in terms of evolution the skills that have become most prized are those related to left-sided functioning in the split brain model as described by Roger Sperry in 1974. This theory, as summarized by Gardner,[7] states that the left side of the brain in right-handed people is the dominant sphere for language acquisition, conceptual functioning, classificatory capabilities, and ultimately reason. The right side of the brain in these same people is responsible for spatial discrimination, musical abilities, artistic gifts, and intuitive abilities. Each side works in concert, and each influences

[5]Herant Katchadourian and John Boli, *Careerism and Intellectualism among College Students* (San Francisco: Jossey-Bass, Inc., 1985), pp. 221–257.
[6]Daniel Offer and Melvin Sabashin, *Normality and the Life Cycle* (New York: Basic Books, 1984), p. 73.
[7]Howard Gardner, *The Minds of New Science* (New York: Basic Books, 1985), p. 275.

profoundly the function of the other. Developmentally, this means that reason, mathematical abilities, decisiveness, and autonomy—all of which are derivatives of left-sided dominance—have highest educational priority, while the right-sided skills which emphasize intuition, artistic traits, and connectedness are less emphasized. The left-sided skills of rationality, decisiveness, coolness, ability to evaluate multiple issues within a relatively brief time period, and ease with mathematical models have achieved eminence as the most desirable traits in an educated person.

The Emergence of Social Cognition

In the relatively near future, many cognitive skills will be duplicated by computers capable of artificial intelligence. These sophisticated machines will take over functions of complicated computation, intricate reasoning, and information classifying, processing, and storage at levels and speed of which human intelligence is incapable. Dependence on the human mind for these tasks will diminish. More importantly, what is presently thought of as non-social cognition—that cognition about ideas, things, natural events, and information—will lose its current preeminence in evolutionary cognition.

The preponderant emphasis on rationality will be replaced by the ascension of social cognition, which consists of information about people—what they do and what they ought to do. This new evolution will be manifested by awareness about the importance of those right-sided skills of perception, intuition, and awareness of feelings. These attributes are essential to the establishment of empathy, the development of judgment, and the accrual of wisdom. Due to prior emphasis on non-social cognitive development and on means of evaluating this through standardized testing, there is, in comparison, insufficient knowledge about both the development of empathy, altruism, friendship, and love and about means of evaluating these traits during development. In addition, the language describing these processes is relatively sparse. To understand these in the detail now accorded to non-social cognition is the next great challenge in development.

In this vein Erik Erikson, author of *Childhood and Society*, a landmark study on the influence of culture on psychosocial development, in an interview with Brenman-Gibson[8] noted that to insure survival in the current nuclear age, reliance on moralism or rules to govern behavior must be replaced by ethics. In this context, ethics—in contrast to morals, which involve obedience to generally accepted rules—are based on insight into human values. They are, therefore, based on choice governed by empathy and concern rather than obedience to rules. This ethical understanding of human values is based on the capacity for empathy, the development of which is pivotal to the successful negotiation of adolescence.

Empathy and Friendship

During childhood young people begin to acquire, in the family and in the neighborhood, the rudiments of understanding about the mutuality of communication between people who care for each other. This knowledge grows in sophistication with maturation and culminates in the capacity for empathy during adolescence. Empathy can be thought of as the capacity of two people to acquire, evaluate, and respond to mutually shared knowledge. Prerequisites for this understanding are autonomy, interest in the social world, and the ability to form friendships. These prerequisites are learned in late childhood and early adolescence as follows.

Friendships and meaningful social relationships in childhood are governed by rules, shared activities, parental acceptance of playmates, and group activities. These could be characterized as somewhat surface activities based on cooperation, the most common form of relationship during childhood. As such, they do not directly deal with the internal life of another person or persons and do not involve sharing of this internal life between two people. As a child matures and passes into adolescence, information processing about another person passes from surface knowledge of shared activities and rules governing these activities to internal life in which the adolescent begins to perceive and infer an underlying internal and interpersonal reality. These perceptions based on intuition introduce a new form of relationship which will become the hallmark of adolescence: namely,

---

[8]Margaret Brennan-Gibson, "Ericson and the 'Ethics of Survival'," *Harvard Magazine* 87 (Nov.–Dec. 1984), pp. 59–64.

that based on collaboration, a higher and more complex form of interaction.

Furthermore, when this information is acknowledged and shared between two people, the relationship is then based on empathy. As stated earlier, empathy forms the beginnings of a higher form of friendship than that found in childhood. In this regard, Shantz[9] defines this new form of friendship as "accepting each other as equals, sharing thoughts and feelings, helping each other with issues of living, and avoiding causing each other problems." Friendships have their beginnings with empathy, progress to an altruistic relationship where the welfare of another is put ahead of the self temporarily, and end with a complementary relationship in which two people seek to evoke the best from each other. Friendships based on complementation are characterized by mutual satisfaction, self-definition, and fulfillment, and include friendships which are equal, platonic, and altruistic. When a person has achieved the capacity for complementation by establishing these types of aforementioned relationships in which empathy and equality are paramount characteristics, the next step in the evolution of relationships is that based on genuine intimacy, which combines all of the preceding qualities of attachment but in addition contains a gradually increasing degree of exclusivity and fidelity.

The Sexuality Factor

Although the majority of relationships among adolescents are more supportive than stressful, burgeoning sexuality during this period of life introduces a qualitatively different and potentially more stressful subset of relationships. Harry Stack Sullivan, as quoted in Goethals,[10] made the prescient observation that competing dynamisms, lust and the need for intimacy, form parallel paths during adolescent development but are united in adulthood by a reciprocal love relationship. To reach this goal, adolescents have diverse relationships—

---

[9]C.V. Shantz, "Social Cognition," in *Handbook of Child Psychology: Cognitive Development*, Vol. 3, J.H. Flavell and E.M. Markman, eds. (New York: J.H. Wiley & Sons, 1983), p. 351.
[10]G.W. Goethals and D.S. Kloss, *Experiencing Youth* (Boston: Little, Brown and Co., 1970), pp. 13–16.

some clearly sexual, others predominantly companionable as outlined in the preceding paragraphs. Young people need a variety of relationships: some encounters that are sexual, some friendships that are relatively free of sexual tension, a few with elements of both, and— of equal importance—some special idealized relationships. Within this range of relationships most teenagers see sexuality as an important but not the most crucial issue.

In support of this, Offer's data[11] indicate that most young people are not afraid of their sexuality and deny that it is more difficult for them to handle sexual feelings and impulses than other strong feelings. There are no firm data to indicate conclusively that young people of recent generations—the popularly termed "sexual revolution" notwithstanding—are more permissive in regard to sexual mores, lose their virginity earlier, and exploit their partners with greater frequency than preceding generations. The picture of permissive and promiscuous adolescents that occasionally emerges in the popular press is once again more of a projection of adult concerns and envy than the actual lifestyle of most adolescents. Adolescents view sex openly, acknowledge its importance, but deny that it is an unsurmountable issue.

There are, however, adolescents for whom sexuality is a major problem. These young people may respond to parental ambivalence expressed by making sex mysterious, designating it as the central aspect of lovability, or equating it inevitably with exploitation or pregnancy by either flaunting sexual behavior or by withdrawing from intimate relationships. More specifically, some young men equate sexual precocity with manly risk-taking and fail to see the narcissistic implications of this type of behavior. Their female counterparts respond to sexual impulses as a means of assuring their acceptability and popularity. Other young people use sexuality as a means of remaining distant, recognizing that it is easy to become sexually involved without any passion or commitment in today's climate. This form of emotional or spiritual apathy may be common among some young people, but not to the extent that it is popularly portrayed.

In summary, most adolescents view sexuality with pleasure, deny that it has greater importance than other issues, and have not responded to the relative sexual permissiveness of the culture with an

---

[11] Daniel Offer *et al.*, *The Adolescent: A Psychological Self-Portrait* (New York: Basic Books, 1981), pp. 61–64.

increase in exploitive behavior. In an article some years ago the present author[12] indicated that chastity as the ideal virtue in young
women had been replaced by that of fidelity to a partner. This new
ideal means that a woman is judged by two criteria: how she handles
what she does do rather than what she does not do, and the effort and
constancy with which she invests an important intimate relationship.
Following this model, men may be judged by the constancy, care, and
consideration they show to a partner rather than by sexual conquest
and performance in multiple relationships. In both sexes, constancy
and fidelity are more important aspects of a sexual relationship than
are gratification and performance.

Sexuality has received disproportionate attention as a major problem in adolescent development. It can be a major problem, but it is
one that all too often masks other issues—for example, neglect, pov-
erty, low parental status, loneliness, parental conflict, poor self-esteem, or alienation. In Goethals' terms, "All too often it (sexuality) is
the rug under which problems of autonomy and identity are swept."[13]

Issues of Gender

In the preceding paragraph, distinctions between men and women
were made in regard to sexuality. Classically, these issues of sexuality
have been afforded more attention than issues involving gender. But,
becoming comfortable with one's own gender and accepting fully in
all its ramifications is of equal importance in adolescence. Traditionally, distinctions between men and women have been made on the basis of what can be thought of as gender exaggeration. In this model
the role differences between the sexes are typed as quite distinct.
Men are typed as rational, non-self disclosing, decisive, risk-taking,
cool and deliberate, task-oriented, and affiliative. In contrast, women
are perceived as emotional, intuitive and perceptive, dependent on
accepting relationships, self-disclosing, nuturant, indecisive, non-
risk-taking, and connected. In short, the majority of the traits which
are considered most desirable by the culture have been ascribed to

---

[12]Paul A. Walters, Jr., "Promiscuity in Adolescence," *The American Journal of Or-
thopsychiatry*, 35 (July 1965), pp. 670–675.
[13]G.W. Goethals and D.S. Kloss, *Experiencing Youth* (Boston: Little, Brown and
Co., 1970), p. 314.

men, and those considered less essential have been granted to women. The origins of this cultural sexism are multiple and not within the purview of this chapter. The resulting stereotypes, however, can be summarized by what Parsons[14] has termed the instrumentative orientation of men and the expressive aspect of women. In this concept men are the "shakers and the movers" and women are the caretakers and the tenders of social custom. It is clear that this simplistic formulation describes neither men nor women in their respective lives as lived.

The women's movement of the sixties established the obvious truism that men and women are more alike than different. In other words, this form of sex role typing was a move away from the traditional method of emphasizing the differences between sexes to a new stance of focusing on similarities between them as people, independent of gender, and on differences among individual men and individual women rather than traits that distinguish men and women. This concept of similarities among the sexes was termed androgeny. The theory states that sex role typing is not bipolar and prescribed by the culture, but that it rests on a balance of endogenous traits acceptable to the individual and those in his or her immediate social radius. Good adaptation is thus related to what is an acceptable balance within the individual. For example, men and women are equally loving, contain the same potential for rational disclosure, have the same need for decisiveness, enjoy risk-taking, are task-oriented, and prefer to be in a relationship rather than unconnected. The issue is not which trait belongs to whom, but rather what is the balance of these traits that is acceptable to the individual, to those he or she loves, and in the social radius.

With varying degrees of comfort, most young people have accepted the fact that there are very few tasks traditionally done by men which cannot be equally well done by women. This basic axiom has been accepted with varying degrees of comfort and optimism by both sexes. In summary, what is beginning to crystallize out of almost twenty years of changes in sex role typing is that the primary differences between the two sexes seem to be in the area of relationships.

---

[14]Talcott Parsons and Gerald Platt, *A Sociology of Age* (New Brunswick, N.J.: Rutgers University Press, 1969).

Friends and Lovers

The path followed by each sex in the establishment of the capacity for attachment, friendship, and intimacy is subtly but unmistakably different. In the emotional development of men, a prominent theme involves the issue of imposed separation and distance from the primary caregiver. For example, early in development men and women are equally close to their mothers. Prior to beginning school and thereafter, men are taught to separate and distance themselves from their mothers and the home as a prerequisite for manliness. In contrast, women have no such requirement. As a result of this emphasis on autonomy over connectedness, men substitute the more distant forms of relating such as bonding, identification, and affiliation for true intimacy and connectedness until late adolescence. This does not mean that men value relationships less; it means, instead, that the capacity for intimacy is slower to develop in men than in women and that their style of relating is more distant and nondisclosing than that of women. According to recent developmental theory, therefore, what distinguishes men and women essentially are not traits as much as styles of relating. Women remain more easily connected, make decisions based on maintaining important relationships, and prefer ongoing intimacy in their lives. In contrast, men may put rational decisions ahead of a relationship, make more superficial friendships in comparison with women, and tend to deny the importance of intimacy in their life until early adulthood.

With these constraints, men were more comfortable in the more distant past when the culture was predominantly homosocial. Friendships and affiliations in daily life were, for the most part, devoted to shared competencies and interests and thus were related to work. Intimacy was found with a partner, usually a wife, or with a few close friends, but the focus of a man's daily life was first his work, and then his family. As Gilligan[15] has noted, these priorities for men worked as long as women were willing to order their life cycle around the family first and a relationship second. Traditionally women have acted as the caretakers of relationships within the culture, while men have been the providers. This form of asymmetry between the sexes worked as

---

[15]Carol Gilligan, *In a Different Voice* (Cambridge, Mass.: Harvard University Press, 1982), pp. 8–23.

long as the culture supported it and the family was organized around it.

In recent years, however, there have been sweeping changes in the roles of both men and women. The women's movement has made strides in blunting discrimination toward women based on traditional sexual stereotypes. In some ways, each sex now has more freedom: women, to pursue the most attractive career to them; and men to be rid of the necessity of being the sole provider.

However laudatory these changes may be, they have changed the face of adolescent development. First of all, the broader culture has become more a heterosocial one in which the sexes mingle in diverse relationships—business, social, intimate, friendships, lovers—without the boundaries of sex role differentiation. Because of their relatively greater interpersonal sophistication, women are able to deal with the diversity of relationships more equitably than men. Women can envision having a career, a marriage, and a family—although the latter with more difficulty—and making them all work. Men, on the other hand, are less certain about the constancy of intimacy in the press of dual careers, and feel somewhat pessimistic about raising children around the demands of work. Their lack of sophistication about the simple fact that if two people care, it will work out, hampers them.

Maintaining Self-Esteem

In this atmosphere of uncertainty, each sex needs to prepare itself for the exigencies of changed relationships. For the sexes to be able to complement each other, they need diversity in relationships during adolescent development. Men need more opportunity for collaborative and noncompetitive closeness. Women, on the other hand, need mentoring and instructions in affiliation, competition, and bonding. The models for all this diversity should be found in the schools, where as much attention has to be paid to the formation of relationships as to cognitive tasks. There is a surprisingly large literature in the teaching of social skills to children which has been summarized by Shantz.[16] There is, however, less attention devoted to the formal

---

[16]C.V. Shantz, "Social Cognition," in *Handbook of Child Psychology: Cognitive Development*, Vol. 3, J.H. Flavell and E.M. Markman, eds. (New York: J.H. Wiley & Sons, 1983), p. 351.

teaching of social skills to adolescents. Klerman[17] made the observation that, as adolescence becomes more prolonged, attachments and the establishment of a social network are more important. In the opinion of this author, the relative diminution in self-esteem among modern youth is due to the decreased availability of parents, the emphasis on achievement over connectedness, and the lack of community supports due to decreased participation by adults in the daily life of the teenager. To reverse this trend, young people need adults to be available and involved without being intrusive.

Another major internal issue in adolescent development is the formation of the capacity to maintain self-esteem through internal affirmation rather than external supports such as academic achievement, peer popularity, athletic prowess, and other forms of outer affirmation. The present emphasis on achievement as being the most important goal of education is in opposition to this internal process, and it results in many young people basing their self-esteem on these external supports alone rather than in conjunction with relationships. Living up to one's potential and establishing a sense of competence in regard to learning is important, but it is not the most important source of self-esteem. Wylie[18] concluded that self-esteem is not related to one single factor; instead it is related to a congruence of the following factors: favored parental treatment, respected family socioeconomic status, high individual achievement, acceptable body characteristics, and popularity with peers. Of these factors, three involve interactions with significant people as an important source of self-esteem to the individual, rather than achievement, high scores, or special skills.

Making a Permanent Base

Traditionally there has been little disagreement about the importance of relationships in a young person's life. The emphasis in recent years, however, has shifted more to accomplishment and achievement

[17]Gerald L. Klerman, "Adaptation, Depression, and Life Events," in *Adolescent Psychiatry*, Sherman C. Feinstein *et al.*, Eds. (Chicago, Ill.: Univ. Chicago Press, 1980), pp. 301–309.
[18]Ruth C. Wylie, *The Self-Concept: Revised Edition, Vol. 2, Theory and Research on Selected Topics* (Lincoln, Neb.: University of Nebraska Press, 1978).

as being more crucial in adolescent passage than the quality of relationships. That message may have been needed following the cultural turmoil of the sixties. It is, however, overemphasized for the eighties and nineties. With social supports and the family in transition and some turmoil, equal emphasis should be placed on attachment and social skills as much as on competency and autonomy.

Hopefully, young people approach puberty with nascent attachment and social skills poised for further development. The foundation for these skills—attachment, empathy, and complementation—is basic trust. Basic trust rests on the conviction that people within the individual's social radius are compassionate and caring. It is the developmental heir to infancy which has been negotiated in a loving atmosphere. Throughout life it will provide the ability to withstand the inevitable pressures of periodic loneliness which will mark an individual's progress through life and to which he is first exposed in full force during adolescence.

During adolescence, loneliness is often the most powerful incentive in the search for new relationships. The first of these new relationships often involves the formation of a collaborative tie with both adults and peers in which mutuality, as measured by empathy and acceptance of others, is paramount. This type of affirmation modifies and confirms ideals to which a young person has aspired. After a time and even concurrently, these collaborative ties are accompanied by another set of connections, complementary attachments in which equality and acceptance of the cared-for individual as a separate person are the main themes. Out of these grow friendships of varying degrees of intensity and of different quality than earlier. Finally, as a result of the diversity of attachments, a young person arrives at the threshold of adulthood having a potential capacity for intimacy in which sexuality, exclusivity, fidelity, and reciprocity are the key elements. This final step is a key one. It enables the young adult to put aside the family of origin and begin to plan the creation of a family of choice, which initially consists of another person with whom genuine intimacy is achieved. In summary, for optimal maturation during adolescence a young person needs diversity of relationships: people like him or her who confirm the self; people to be admired who lead the self toward union with the ideal self; and, finally, people to love who affirm the real self.

Conclusion

In this chapter the interplay between external forces and internal developmental issues has been considered in light of the evolutionary relationship between new emphases in the development of the self, on the one hand, and the demands of the culture on the other. The most important external forces reside first in the family, from whom the adolescent receives values, and next in the school, from which he or she obtains direction. Internally, developmental changes in cognition and sex role elaboration furnish motivation to act in one's own behalf. From the congruence of all of these—family values, cultural expectations, and personal motivations—self-esteem is firmed and the young person becomes able to act on ambitions and be guided by ideals. All of these components act in consonance to form an identity which is subject to further modification throughout life. At varying times, some of these components may be stronger, further ahead in regard to maturational goals, or even discordant temporarily. For successful adaptation, however, consonance and continuity between them are more important than the development of single strengths. Like an orchestra, the firmness of the self lies in its ability to combine component parts rather than individual solos. In the adolescent, therefore, adaptation is measured by connectedness as well as autonomy, androgenous sex role traits as well as bipolar ones, and empathy as well as rationality.

Chapter 4

THE EFFECT OF PERSONAL FEELINGS ON COUNSELING STUDENTS

Douglas H. Powell

> *"I've just flunked the biology midterm because I didn't study,"* sobs
> a 14-year-old, *"and I guess that means I'm never going to be a doctor.
> My father always had his heart set on my going to medical school.
> What am I going to do?"*
>
> *"My boyfriend and I have started sleeping together,"* says an at-
> tractive sophomore. *"I know we shouldn't, but we are so much in love
> and we just can't keep our hands off each other. What do you think?"*
>
> When you order a group of boys to turn down their stereo, their
> response is: *"Why are you always picking on us? Can't we listen to a
> little music?"* When they are told to turn down the stereo right now,
> the music diminishes, but you hear a familiar voice refer to you as an
> *"F—ing A—hole."*
>
> *"It's a mystery to me why any intelligent person with an ounce of
> ambition would teach,"* sneers a chronic underachieving advisee. *"Do
> you ever feel you've totally wasted your life?"*

Comments such as these from students can arouse powerful affects in
us—sympathy, lust, anger, despair. These emotions can make it extremely difficult to sit with troubled students, to hear their problems,
or to help them because we are so overpowered by the inner feelings
their actions trigger within us. In this context, the first few minutes
of an encounter with a troubled student are critical in setting the tone

69

for the counseling relationship. In these early moments we can demonstrate to students that we can hear their distress, and they will sense our empathy and compassion. Conversely, we can destroy the potential for developing a trusting rapport in the first 120 seconds of our contact with a young man or young woman if we allow our own needs and values, conflicts and unfinished business from our own adolescence, or our unique vulnerabilities to block our ability to listen.

Counseling is far more a process than an outcome. Many times we do not know why a student is upset and has fallen into a slump. Or we know that the upset has occurred because the parents have separated, but we feel powerless to help in the face of the youngster's overwhelming grief. Or, we have no idea what to tell someone for whom everything seems to have lost its meaning. Or, finally, we see the problem, know the cause, and tell the young person what to do, only to find our most considered wisdom rejected out of hand. Yet, it is not unusual for young people to benefit greatly from these encounters with us. For it is our capacity to listen, far more than the ability to point them in the right direction, that is the essence of an effective helping relationship.

Let us look first at some of the factors which limit our ability to share the experience of a student. These include our own needs, generational contrasts in life-cycle tasks, illusions about teenagers, and our unique vulnerabilities. Then we shall make some suggestions which might be helpful in recognizing and minimizing the effect of these limiting factors on the counseling relationship.

The Teacher's Needs

Teaching young people is an enormously gratifying occupation, partly because it gives us an opportunity to fulfill so many of our own needs. These include the need to be right, the need to be in control, the need to guide, the need to have a close relationship with the younger generation, and the need to fulfill the rescue fantasy. Most of us in related helping professions share these needs.

A large part of what makes the careers of many teachers enjoyable is the opportunity to exhibit their superior knowledge and confidence. Nothing pleases them more than posing questions and helping youngsters find the right answers, be it making sense of poetry, the scientific method, the mysteries of irregular verbs, or quadratic equations. The need to be right often extends into areas beyond the classroom. These teachers enjoy engaging students in discussions on nearly any subject—drugs, gay rights, the national debt, what to do in Central America—and then demonstrating that they know the correct answer.

Then there are faculty who are drawn to teaching because they are in complete charge of a small portion of the universe: their campus and their classroom. Within these boundaries they set the rules, decide what material will be emphasized, create a climate in which learning will occur, regulate the pace of instruction, and dispense rewards and punishments as they choose. They are motivated by a sense of influencing the growth of the younger generation in directions consonant with their views of the right way. In no other sphere of their lives are they so much in charge.

Closely related is the gratification that comes from guiding the next generation, shaping what they think, feel, and do. Much of what many teachers find satisfying about education is directing youngsters toward experiences they believe to be best. They enjoy recommending books and movies. They love to discuss students' emotional reactions to someone who is strange, a girlfriend at another school, or which college is best. They recommend playing soccer, going out for the spring musical, or trying Outward Bound. For them the bottom line is telling young people what will be in their best interest.

Then there are some men and women for whom a primary motivating force is having special friends in the student body. They form close attachments in the course of coaching them in a sport, dramatics, or debate; working with them as student leaders; or participating in school activities such as trips to Europe or hiking on the Appalachian Trail. They find themselves able to share comfortably their deepest, most personal ideas and emotions with students, and find their openness reciprocated. Graduation is a terrible wrench for these teachers. It is not uncommon to find students at secondary schools who have been the special beneficiaries of very close and intimate relationships with teachers.

The rescue fantasy is deeply rooted in many faculty members. Briefly defined, it is the need to save a student from what they perceive to be a highly dangerous and threatening situation. Such action is beyond a teacher's usual empathic reaching out to someone in trouble; rather, it is the perception that a young person's distress is of potentially life-threatening—or, at least, happiness-threatening—

proportions. Ordinary understanding and help are therefore not enough. A full-fledged rescue effort is required to salvage this youngster by force of the teacher's intervention.

Experience generally reduces these needs to realistic dimensions. We recognize that our students also obtain input about what is right from other teachers and adults in their lives and that this information may be at odds with what we tell them. We also accept the reality that our school controls only a fraction of their lives. There will be other influences which will dilute our efforts and frustrate our best intentions to provide an optimal atmosphere for their development. As we see them forming solid relationships among their peers, finding a best friend, and falling in love, we realize that affection invested in building these affiliative bonds must necessarily be subtracted from their expressions toward us. And we discover that not all students who seem to be in need of being saved will allow us to help them, and that some will resolutely cling to their unhappiness, resisting all our efforts to help them feel better. And nothing dire apparently happens to them.

Teachers who counsel when they have inadequate insight into their own needs find that they have limited ability to listen to students, to share their problems, and to help them find a way to relieve their distress. The teacher's unresolved feelings well up reflexively, causing him or her to interrupt, chastize, criticize, and to direct rather than to listen. For example:

> *"If you had listened to me when I told you not to take honors biology, you wouldn't be having this problem."*

> *"You know, you're spending too much time with your new friends who I warned you about. They're a bad influence. None of them care how they do in school."*

Most teachers who work with young people have made these automatic responses to their pain. Instead of hearing what is being said by the student, they listen to an inner voice.

Generational Contrast in Life Cycle Tasks

It is said that the two worst times of a woman's life are when she turns thirteen and when her daughter turns thirteen. The truth of this somewhat sexist statement lies in the recognition that much of what makes it difficult for the older generation is that they must struggle with the challenges of their own stage in the life cycle while trying to help their students cope with the developmental issues of childhood and adolescence. The life cycle problems of faculty members stand in sharp contrast to the developmental tasks confronting the student body. For example, one component of normal adaptation is being able to find satisfaction from a balance of working, loving, and playing. The ingredients of such a balance, however, are far different for adults, on the one hand, and for students, on the other.

Adults need to feel productive and generative in their work. Visualize this scene: A middle-age science teacher is the mother of three and works a minimum of 70 hours a week. She exercises regularly at a health club and is thinking of running for the town finance committee. She comes upon a talented ninth grade girl who is lackadaisical, disorganized, unprepared for classes, and owes 14 lab assignments. The student seems to exist on a special diet of root beer, barbecued potato chips, and candy bars. She cheerfully acknowledges that she hates school and does not care about anything else either.

We can only imagine the kneejerk reactions this teacher may have as she contrasts her advisee's situation to her own. Some of the more likely outcomes might be anger at the disparity in her output of energy and that of the student; irritation over the girl's lack of concentration; and frustration over her apparent lack of commitment and self-discipline. The faculty member's feelings may prevent her from recalling some fundamental things that she otherwise would be aware of: It is far easier to devote energy to activities that are congenial than those that are not; two decades of being yoked to tasks that force us to groove our work habits enables us to do things that we do not want to do without undue struggle; and commitment and enthusiasm usually come only when we have a reasonably clear sense of what we want to do with our lives.

As adults we have the need to feel generative too. An essential part of feeling creative and productive in our work is the belief that we are improving the generation which follows. We have a natural wish to pass on our values, ideas, and accumulated wisdom. So, how does it affect us when teenagers reject our ideals as the first step toward discovering their own? In the course of their own maturation they may disparage the lifestyle we have labored and sacrificed to construct, reject the advice we give them, and proclaim their own rule: Whoever has the gold makes the rules. These attitudes can be infuriating to adults who are committed to the values of service, morality, integrity, and loyalty. Overburdened adults also are provoked by youngsters who are insensitive to the adults' own struggles and problems, who seem to care only for themselves, and who do little or nothing to contribute to the community.

It is likewise difficult for teachers at middle age not to resent students who have more money than they need and who make outlandish requests. Consider, for example, the student who asked to borrow $150 to rent a limo to go to a concert because his parents were skiing in Gstaad and thus unavailable—just when the teacher was wondering where to get money to have the ominous sounds eliminated from the transmission of the family automobile. Or, a teacher may come dangerously close to losing control when, after spending an evening counseling her mother in Phoenix about her father's creeping Alzheimer's and commiserating with her son in Schenectady who has just been laid off, she finds lying in wait outside the classroom door at 7:45 a.m. an extraordinarily self-centered 15-year-old boy who wants to tell her for the twentieth time about a girlfriend who broke up with him. Or, a teacher may have trouble controlling his feelings when a boy on the way to class tramples through a flower bed he carefully planted outside a classroom building, when a girl can't carry out a 10-minute work detail because she fears destroying a fresh manicure, or when an 11th grade proctor leaves a trail of candy wrappers across the school grounds.

The final arena in which developmental issues of the generations conflict is play. Play, in the words of Mark Twain's *Tom Sawyer,* is "what a body is *not* obliged to do." It is also an activity we do not have to do particularly well and in which we can follow changing whims, and it is present-oriented. Part of the problem between the generations arises from a misunderstanding of what play is. Most youngsters understand it instinctively. But a coach seeing a girl with a natural facility at tennis may believe it is the girl's "moral obligation" to develop her aptitude to the fullest. "Anything worth doing is worth doing well," he will say. After all, that is what he would do if he had it to do over again, he thinks. He will encourage her to practice regularly, accept private coaching, and play—if that is the word—in competition. If her interests begin to flag or she wants to try lacrosse, he will be horrified: "But you have a God-given talent for tennis, and you must use it!" We are all too familiar with the teenager who gives up a sport because the adults around him or her are excessively zealous in their encouragement and support. As one veteran sports official put it, "Whenever some coaches see a spark of ability, they drench it with their own enthusiasm."

Misconceptions about Teenagers

Excessive responses by adults are, from time to time, conditioned by pre-existing beliefs as to what adolescents are "really" like. A 13-year-old boy comes to school in a leather jacket, combat boots, and cartridge belt, and he refuses to change clothes. A teacher wants to say, "I won't have you looking like that! Take those clothes off this instant!" The source of this overreaction has little to do with the notion that the boy looks like a fool in that garb; rather, it emanates from a number of subconscious fantasies sometimes harbored by adults about adolescents.

The belief that adolescents are out of control and are therefore dangerous and to be feared is common in those who work with them. As puberty transforms weak and malleable children into strong and independent youth who increasingly wish to control portions of their lives, adults may misread their pursuit of autonomy as a threat. We become angry because a young man's outfit seems to defy our authority. Or, subconsciously we fear that the young are about to seize power from the older generation—after all, the boy seems dressed for combat.

A second source of erratic and excessive reactions is the subconscious anxiety that teenagers will act out our own fantasies, about which we may have considerable inner conflict. Typically we may, for example, have unfinished business involving sexual or aggressive impulses. In such cases we may project our own ambivalent desires onto our students, imagining them to be just as concerned with sexual matters or intimidating people who cross them as we might have been in our own teenage years. In sum, we are likely to give these youngsters very confusing messages. If, for example, we have inner conflicts about our own sexual feelings, we may rage at a 14-year-old girl in a skin-tight outfit, thinking of her as a "little slut" for dressing that way. We may even tell her that she should stop "being so promiscuous," and that she had better learn about birth control techniques. (The girl may, in fact, be barely at the hand-holding stage with the boy, and the only reason she is going to the party is to be with her girlfriends.) Not a few girls have responded to this double message by launching themselves into premature sexual activity, "because if that's what you expect, then I might as well do it."

Another issue is aggression. Generally, secondary school teachers are especially sensitive to overt expressions of physical aggression. Verbal abuse may be tolerated but punching is not. Occasionally, however, a teacher who has had problems with his own frustrated aggression may encourage a boy not to let people push him around, but then overreact when the young man follows his direction.

Unique Vulnerabilities

A teacher's own vulnerabilities may impair his or her ability to hear what a troubled student is saying. These internal patterns range from simple variations in diurnal rhythm to rather complicated feelings about particular types of people, ideas, emotions, interests, or relationships. These patterns affect our mental set and, thus, our ability to enter into the counseling process.

Diurnal rhythms refer to the times of day when we are at our physiological and mental peak and valley. It is no secret that the world is divided into morning people and night people. Some teachers arise before daybreak, get an hour or two of work in before school, and are impatient to get on with the business of the day. They arrive at school feeling good and greet their colleagues and students cheerfully. At 9:00 a.m. they are at the top of their game. By contrast, some faculty only begin to come alive at dusk, functioning best at night. They often stay up until midnight and beyond when they tackle their most challenging tasks.

Paying attention to diurnal variations is beneficial. Knowing when we are at our best enables us to schedule our most taxing challenges during those periods. Advisers who are morning people do well to work with their most difficult students early in the day.

Ignoring one's diurnal cycle can cause one to be notably ineffective. For a time I saw a young man, Ron, at 9:00 a.m. to try to help him with his depressive feeling that his life had no meaning. He kept getting worse despite my efforts over a period of six months, and I had no idea why. All I could think of was that old psychotherapist's joke, "I think I could help you with your depression if everything didn't seem so futile." Then, mysteriously, he began to get better.

Two years after he graduated he invited me to have lunch with him. I was delighted to accept because I genuinely liked him and because had always wondered what happened in our counseling relationship to cause him to improve.

At lunch he said that, during the first six months of our contact, he could barely tolerate talking with me because I seemed so insensitive to his problems. Only inertia, his reluctance to look for another therapist, kept him returning. According to him, I would come bouncing into my office, greet him cheerily, and ask him briskly how he was feeling. To Ron it seemed that I exhibited no sensitivity at all to his despair because my moods were at such odds with his. After six months of therapy, however, my schedule changed so that I had to see him at 4:00 p.m. Things improved then because, at that time of the day, I was at the low ebb of my diurnal cycle. The consequently slower pace of our interviews enabled him to connect with me, and we were able to make some progress in helping him understanding his difficulties.

Our feelings about particular individuals—their situations, attitudes, values, and specific conflicts—may resonate so vigorously with some of our own experiences that we are at risk of losing our objectivity. This is because we are dealing with something within us rather than within them. Psychoanalysts sometimes call this phenomenon "countertransference." For example, because of my own inner conflicts about religion, I do not do particularly well with individuals who have a religious crisis. If we recognize people with particular issues or troubles that mirror our own, it is helpful to refer them to colleagues who are less likely to be in conflict about these matters and who, therefore, will be more sensitive and effective as counselors.

Sometimes teachers' feelings cause them to overidentify with students and make a "safe passage" response to those who somehow remind them of themselves. Two varieties of this response are common. The first is the desire to be certain that a youngster takes advantage of opportunities similar to those which slipped through a teacher's hands when he or she was a student. "Had I studied harder and taken honors courses, I might have gone to Princeton. Had I applied for that Congressional internship between the eleventh and twelfth grades, I might be a lawyer now. Had I kept at basketball and developed a jump shot instead of quitting after the 10th grade, I might have made the varsity team."

A second example of a safe passage response stems from teachers' intense desire to guide students around the particular problems they experienced in their youth. Seeing a bright girl turn away from classroom work, quit the soccer team, and avoid positions of leadership in order to be with marginal friends and date a 19-year-old dropout, or witnessing a nice boy unable to resist the bright lights—including partying, alcohol, and drugs—makes such a teacher physically ill. Why? Because the teacher had identical problems during teenage years and paid a terrible price. Somehow these teachers feel that they *must* get through to this girl and this boy and warn them away from the hazards that will mark their lives forever.

In short, teachers are greatly disturbed when they see students ignoring their advice to seize opportunities or their warnings to avoid certain dangers, choosing instead to make the same wrong turns they made in their youth. The pain caused by these self-defeating choices resonates with their own discomfort a generation or more in the past.

Coping with Vulnerabilities in a Counseling Relationship

The most important message for anyone carrying out the complex business of counseling is Aristotle's maxim, "Know thyself." The unexamined inner life, especially when we try to share the experience of young people, can create a barrier which may frustrate our best efforts to help students. And while the unexamined life can hinder our full professional growth, the examined life may be no bed of roses either. Professional counselors should regularly take an inventory of their own vulnerabilities and weaknesses which may impact their capacity to counsel effectively. They should look at themselves as objectively as possible and, in the light of new developments in their lives, think carefully about individuals with whom they seem to be having trouble and try to discern the extent to which their own feelings may be obscuring their understanding of existing difficulties. This process can be rather painful and humbling.

Ineffective counseling is not generally done by someone incompetent, neurotic, or malicious but by someone overburdened and overextended. There are moments when all of us have had more than we can deal with, are at the wrong phase of our diurnal variation, and cannot cope with one more problem. If, at that moment, a troubled student comes seeking help, it may be necessary to say, "I'm sorry I can't help you right now. I'll be glad to see you tomorrow morning." Or, "I'm sorry I can't see you now. There is simply too much going on in my life. I think you might find it useful to talk to Ms. Jones or Dean Smith. Would you like me to call one of them for you?"

A counselor must avoid certainties of mind about the nature of the student's problem and what should be done about it. Few things are more harmful to initiating a counseling relationship than appearing to know what the problem is and what is causing it before the student states it. For example, "Why are you feeling upset? It's your classmate, isn't it?" Or, "How are you feeling? You look depressed." Or, "What's happening in biology? Are you putting in enough time on your homework?" Having asked a question, one should wait for the answer instead of jumping to a conclusion.

In a counseling relationship, it is important to resist the impulse to do something helpful or to give advice for at least five minutes. Follow the rule, "Don't just *do* something, *stand* there!" How rare it is in the human experience to have someone pay full attention to us—to give us undivided attention for as little as 300 seconds. To have another human being listen to us about our troubles, our concerns, and our conflicts—even for brief moments without telling us their own troubles, expressing their values, making a diagnosis, or giving us advice—is an exceptional event in anyone's life. These moments can be enormously healing even when nothing is said or prescribed.

Being comfortable without immediately knowing the answer to a student's problem or without knowing exactly where you are headed in an encounter with a student or how you are going to get there is part of the art of counseling. The counseling process is not like a cross-examination in a courtroom in which a lawyer asks the question, anticipates the response, and then ripostes with another question, carrying the discussion to a preordained conclusion. Rather, most counseling is a little bit like the way many people play chess: They make a couple of standard opening moves, but from then on it is pure reaction to the other's moves. This may not be the best way to win at chess, but it seems to work in counseling encounters.

One must be careful about making assumptions. The precocious 13-going-on-21-year-old girl who has high school boys lined up in cars waiting for her when an 8th grade class ends may cause you to be certain that she is headed for serious trouble. Or, when you hear that she spent a weekend at a party given by an 11th grader at his parents' ski chalet, you may feel certain that she is sexually active. Driven by these automatic certainties, you may hear yourself thinking things such as, "You're going to get a bad reputation," or "You'd better watch out, or you're going to become pregnant." While it is possible that the 13-year-old is sexually active, the odds are that she is not. Rather, her precocity may cause her to feel that she does not fit in with her less mature classmates, and so she naturally gravitates to older teenagers. But she doubtless feels uncomfortable with this group, too. This discrepancy is what needs to be understood.

Consider how comforting it would be for this student to be asked what it is like to be in an eighth grade class while also receiving attention from older students. It surely must be exciting and flattering. It also could help her to act in a more grownup fashion. But, are there downside aspects? How is she treated by the older girls? To what extent are the interests of juniors and seniors different from her own? Does having friends among high school students affect her relationships with her own classmates?

There are probably few people in her world whom she will be able to talk with about these important matters. If the counselor's openness to these issues is blocked by quick assumptions about the meaning of the student's actions, the ability to share her experience may be forfeited.

Labelling is another pitfall. On the whole, labels tend to obscure more than they reveal. To say that a boy is "lazy" because he is never prepared for history class may overlook the fact that he sings with the concert choir and works fifteen hours a week at a fast food restaurant. If we react to this youngster as though the label assigned him is valid, rather than seeing him as someone for whom other things are demanding his attention more than history, we may condemn him unjustly and write him off rather than understanding his disinclination to pour his energies into a particular intellectual field of interest as a choice he has made. If this occurs, it will not be long before the pupil begins to live down to these expectations.

The correct approach is to find out where the student is allocating his enthusiasm in order to better understand him. Such an objective approach may make it possible to encourage him to invest enough energy in world history that he can get on with the business of advancing his career in other areas.

Another helpful perspective is to try to find something likeable about a troubling student. Few enterprises are more likely doomed to failure than that in which an adviser tries to counsel a student about whom his or her feelings are almost totally negative. Imagine being a female biology teacher, small in stature and controlling by nature, having in your class a rowdy, wisecracking, indolent fullback from the football team. He does not work, makes rude double entendres, and says, "When do we talk about sex in this class?" Not only do you resent his attitude, but his impertinent behavior threatens control of the classroom environment. It is hard for the teacher to like him well enough to try to help him.

Suppose that this teacher could view his behavior as a 15-year-old's attempt to develop a feeling of autonomy by being provocative toward authority figures in school—in this case, the biology teacher. Then, instead of feeling personally challenged and defensive, she might engage him in discussions in which he would be encouraged to debate the opposite side of important issues. In this way the teacher may enable the boy to find a creative rather than a destructive outlet for his oppositional behavior.

The teacher should also scale down rescue fantasies. Most students are not in as much trouble as they appear to be, and the majority of them get better on their own. About 30 percent of troubled young people improve *after* they make an appointment but *before* they see professional counselors for the first time. The stress passes or they figure things out for themselves, and their mood lifts. Also, there are others available to help them—friends, faculty, and parents.

In any case, no one is indispensable. Many counselors have had the experience of becoming ill or having to respond to a family emergency and therefore being unable to meet with students who seem unable to get along without them. Subsequently they find, to their surprise and feeling a slight insult to their pride, that all those apparently dependent students somehow got along perfectly well in their absence. This point is vividly illustrated by the experiences of a psychiatrist who, one Friday afternoon, failed to receive a message from a troubled student which read, "I'm on the roof of your office building, and I have to talk to you now or I'll jump." On Monday morning the doctor finally did receive the message. Quaking, he called the student's number and was relieved to hear the student answer the phone. When the therapist asked him about the message, the student replied, "Well, when you didn't call, I decided I had to figure out things for myself, and so I did. I'll see you Thursday afternoon."

It is important to remain receptive to new developments in the counseling process. One of the more distressing pieces of research data on professional psychotherapists is that, after about the fourth hour of contact, they tend to close their minds to what the problem is and what the contributing factors may be. All counselors share this risk. When the counseling process seems to have come to a halt, it can be that the counselor has closed his or her mimd prematurely to an important aspect of the problem. A good question to ask ourselves when working with somebody over the course of a year is, "What do I know that's new about this individual today?"

Counselors should monitor whether they are getting too close to students. One can recognize this condition when a student begins to be on one's mind all the time or in one's dreams. Being too close is expressed by an increasingly strong desire to share aspects of one's own life with them, paying excessive attention to one's attire when meeting with them or being excessively hurt when they do not show up for a meeting. Other evidence of too much closeness is when contact with students becomes so important that it compromises the teacher's time with friends, spouses, children, and colleagues.

We should remember that what seems to help individuals is not the technique we master in counseling or the advice that we give them. Unlike our colleagues in other aspects of education, we do not have computer-assisted instruction, self-paced learning, overhead projectors, VCR's, or lightweight, high-strength equipment. All we have is ourselves. It is in our willingness to give our attention to students that often makes such a difference in their lives. A sincerely offered hand, ear, and heart are hard to resist.

Counselors should avoid dire predictions. Most troubled adolescents turn out to be productive, normally functioning adults—to the astonishment of many of their teachers. Physical maturation, life experiences, the development of effective ways of managing stress, a satisfying job, the affection of loved ones, as well as the fact that the world beyond the school is far easier for many to manage, combine to enable the majority of our underachieving, disruptive, and troubled students to look astonishingly sound when they return for their reunions.

Therefore, beware of telling the boy with 1400 SAT's but C− grades that he's doomed to a life of frustration unless he lives up to his aptitudes. The disorganized, never-prepared, and inattentive girl should not be condemned to selling clothes in a discount store unless she shapes up. Nor does a D+ in biology necessarily mean that a freshman's dream of being a doctor has gone up in smoke. In sum, teachers must avoid reacting out of anxiety and the desire to change students before the worst happens to them. Predicting the worst in the hope of shaking students out of their apathy or frightening them into disciplined study can be like throwing dynamite on an oil fire to extinguish it. When done by an expert it is sometimes effective; when done by those who are not expert, it usually spreads the conflagration.

*   *   *

When I visit a school I frequently find myself speculating about the graduates whose names are attached to the science building, the new athletic fields, or the arts center. How many of them, I wonder, were given by those in that half of the class that made the top half possible? A large proportion, I suspect. The reason is that these individuals, who experienced academic, behavioral, or psychological problems as students, survived to move on to the next phases of their life cycle, and they are enormously grateful and loyal to their institutions. And most often the reason for their survival is that somewhere along the line a member of the faculty was able to reach out to these troubled youngsters, share their experience, and make a difference.

Chapter 5

TEACHING COUNSELING TO TEACHERS

Janet Sand

For 25 years, members of the Northfield-Fountain Valley Counseling Institutes have been teaching counseling to secondary school teachers in week-long residential institutes and in briefer faculty workshops. In doing so, we act on our beliefs that counseling is an appropriate arena for teachers and that we can prepare teachers to enter that arena in a rather brief time. As both of these beliefs can certainly be questioned, I would like to address the issues of *why* counseling skills are helpful to teachers before discussing *how* to teach them.

Teachers as Counselors

The simplest and clearest statement of purpose came from a Northfield participant, a teacher named Connie Carlie, who said, "They're talking to you anyway." This fact is the first reason to support counseling in schools by teachers. Teachers are very important in the lives of young people. It matters to a student what their teachers think of them—whether a teacher thinks that a student has potential, is trustworthy, is a person of goodwill. In early childhood, the development of self-esteem is centered in the home and requires the loving approval of one's parents. As the child moves out into the world, he is exposed to the judgment of peers and adults in other spheres, and his self-judgment must take account of their view of him. The adolescent is in the process of developing a sense of himself in the world that can stand separate from his parents' judgment, that will allow him to make his own way with a stable feeling of self-worth that does not need constant glory and success and that can integrate the experience of failure and disappointment. Teachers, non-parental adults, provide a bridge from parents out into the world. They help students to see their parents as adults with particular personalities and viewpoints among other adults, in similarity or contrast to their teachers. A teacher who cares for a student, but without the intense investment of a parent, can be a sounding board for the student who is struggling with the adolescent task of making up one's mind and the accompanying fear of being alone in the world. When students' homes are troubled, teachers can provide stability and sanctuary. Teachers stand *between*—between the love from one's parents and the judgment from the working world, between the intense concern of parents with one's actions and choices and the adult world where one must choose for oneself.

Young people to whom teachers do not matter have already been failed by adults. They enter their own adulthoods handicapped, not only because of a lack of guidance but because adulthood, which they are destined to enter, holds negative values and meanings. Students pay attention to teachers, and their interactions—forced or voluntary—are opportunities for positive or negative encounters, depending in large measure on whether the student feels heard. Whether a teacher consciously attends to the emotional communication from her students or not, whether she wishes them to present her with some of the issues and dilemmas they bring, "they're talking to you anyway." And students are more likely to express their concerns to teachers— directly or in code, in language or behavior—than to make an appointment with the school psychologist.

In everyday life with students, a teacher often knows a great deal about the students' emotional lives—who is confident, who is shy, who has been rejected by the college of her choice, who has recently become sullen, whose work is going downhill, who has become much more put-together and mature than he was two years ago, whose father has just died—to others she seems untouched. The issue is not whether a teacher should know about a student's emotional life, but in what way the teacher will respond.

The second major reason to support counseling in schools by teachers is that feeling and thinking are inextricably bound together. A student's capacity to learn material is affected by myriad emotional events, states, meanings. Examples abound. A depressed student cannot motivate himself to read the material, or, if he does, he cannot remember it. An anxious student memorizes formulas for days, but her mind becomes a blank during the exam. A student in conflict with his successful, hard-driven, often absent, accountant father finds himself unable to pass math. The top girl science student in seventh grade refuses to take advanced placement chemistry in tenth because the other students are "nerds."

The preoccupied self-consciousness of teenagers, especially in middle school years, can make sitting and listening and studying and learning adult-generated material painfully difficult, either fraught with too much meaning for the achievement-driven student or lacking in meaning entirely for the student concerned primarily and desperately with his place in the social hierarchy of his peers. Humans are makers of meaning, and learning in school offers multiple opportunities. The subject matter, grades, classmates, parental expectations, and one's relationship with the teacher all have meaning and generate feelings which enhance or interfere with learning. The teacher, already in a relationship with a student, is often on the scene to see the first evidence of that student's distress. I remember two students at the very end of a semester, each bogged down in a paper and unable to complete it. This young man and young woman were good students, but each was hopelessly trying to work harder and harder, generating reams of material and letting other work slide until that, too, was in jeopardy. Each student was brought to this impasse by totally different emotional reasons. They consulted me only after repeated trials at the task, numerous consultations with the teacher, and attempted help from friends had failed, finally leading them to seek a psychologist with a plea for help in the belief that the interference might be emotional. The teacher who is willing to consider and to engage in discussion of the emotional field can often help the student realize much sooner the impact of feelings and can help to avoid the distress and damage to self-esteem of behavior that one cannot understand or control.

The teacher is *on the scene* to see the student's struggles with the paper, to hear the star athlete's resignation from the team, to encounter the student in the hall sobbing to a friend. The opportunity to be present and to be helpful in these situations is available to the teacher in a special role that is not available to many, including the professional psychotherapist in the consulting room whose clients must identify themselves as needing psychological counseling. Most counseling opportunities left unidentified or untended do not lead to the therapist's office or to tragic consequences, but they do remain missed opportunities for connection and growth.

Preparing Teachers for the Counseling Role

I have long had the conviction—some might say it was an obsession— that the therapeutic relationship is only a special instance of inter- personal relationships in general, and that the same lawfulness gov- erns all such relationships. (Carl Rogers)[1]

There is a story in which someone asks a famous sculptor how he cre- ates his masterpieces. He replies that he sees what is in the marble, and that he merely cuts away what should not be there. This is in many ways the task of teaching counseling: to help teachers *stop* doing what interferes with the counseling process and to give them confidence that what is essential is already within their experience.

Teachers who wish to counsel students are a self-selected group. They have chosen to work with—and, often, in boarding schools, to live with—young people rather than to build houses or to be invest- ment bankers. Of that group of teachers, those interested in coun- seling want particularly to have something to do with their students' emotional lives. Schools select those teachers to attend institutes or workshops who are expected to make good use of counseling skills. Some are teachers who are sought out by students because of their personal styles and interpersonal skills. Others occupy positions con- cerned with administrative, coaching, dorm life, and other spheres surrounding that of academic performance.

A master's program in counseling takes one to two years and doc- toral studies require four to five years, yet we confidently offer week- long institutes or visit schools for even shorter workshops. What can we presume to teach of value in such a short time? In some ways, our goals are rather limited—and we meet them. We do not expect to transform people. We expect them to remain quite themselves,

---

[1]Carl R. Rogers, *On Becoming a Person* (Boston: Houghton Mifflin, 1961), p. 39.

counseling very much in their own usual styles. The talkers will talk, the controllers will try to control, the optimists and the pessimists will be optimistic and pessimistic. What we hope for and expect is that the participants will feel empowered to take chances, to ask the next question, to allow the necessary silence, and to listen for and value feelings, both their students' and their own.

Good counseling skills are good interpersonal skills. In general, teachers who are good counselors already have and value skills in relationships before they decide to "learn counseling." What we are doing is not training counselors but helping teachers develop a counseling attitude—an orientation toward listening more than telling, toward feelings more than "facts." Indeed, as Preston Munter says, paraphrasing Dr. Farnsworth, "In counseling, feelings *are* the facts."

The primary aim in helping teachers to counsel students is fostering attitudes rather than teaching techniques. Many studies on counseling and psychotherapy[2] find that a cluster of variables is of central importance in determining which helping relationships are most effective. What is especially interesting is that these "counselor" variables concern not technique or theoretical background but essentially attitudes—that is, how the counselor experiences the situation in a way that leads naturally to appropriate action. Certainly healthier people often make better progress in counseling than those with serious and chronic difficulty, but the counselors who have better outcomes within each group tend to be those who exhibit greater warmth, genuineness, and empathy.

The most effective counselors are the most warm and accepting, showing unconditional positive regard of the counselee. As humans with our own past experiences, we certainly have attitudes and beliefs about how people should feel and behave. But although no one experiences perfect unconditional positive regard for every other person, the most helpful counselors attempt to understand others in a personal idiosyncratic way rather than seeing them as a type or trying to fit them into a theory. They care in a way that is neither possessive nor judgmental.

The better counselors are the most genuine—that is, they know what they feel and there is congruence between their feelings and their awareness of them. Whether a counselor shares his feelings di-

---

[2]C. B. Truax and R. R. Carkhoff, *Toward Effective Counseling and Psychotherapy* (Chicago: Aldine, 1967).

rectly with the counselee depends on the situation, but he must know them himself and not act in contradiction to them.

Empathy is the third central variable; the ability of the counselor to sense what the counselee is feeling and to communicate that perception to the counselee. It is the wish to get in the student's shoes, to see it as he or she does. When we speak of warmth, genuineness, and empathy, we are not describing some aquarian sentimentality. We all like to think of ourselves as caring, concerned, helpful people, and we avoid knowing when we are otherwise. It is difficult—at times painfully so—to allow ourselves to become aware of our own tendencies to judge our counselees, to acknowledge our own negative or erotic feeling for them, or to realize that we may be responding to our own feelings when we thought we were so attuned to theirs.

In the counseling relationship, whether on the run or in the office, whether in a single encounter or several over time, one's *self*—one's feelings, one's knowledge, one's past experience—is the only tool one has. The more one knows not only about how people work—the psychology and sociology of adolescence, for example—but most especially about oneself, the more effective an instrument one can be. How can this best be done? The central goal of teaching counseling must be, as much as one is able, to provide a human environment for teachers learning counseling that is warm, genuine, and empathically attuned so that their feelings are honored and their growth fostered.

A Teaching Model

The Northfield-Fountain Valley Counseling Institutes provide one model for teaching counseling, a time-limited intensive residential workshop combining teachers from many different schools. (In fact, no more than two faculty members from any one school can attend the same institute, and they are never placed in the same small group.) Although this is the model that best suits us in terms of our resources and goals, all programs have constraints. Other settings may lose the intensity of the personal experience in the introduction to counseling but offer more opportunities for training and support over time. Let us begin with a description of the Northfield-Fountain Valley model and later discuss essential central features of program teaching counseling.

Although the week-long residential institute can be seen as having some characteristics of a school or even of a summer camp, it is in many senses designed as a retreat, a place of withdrawal from everyday pressures and responsibilities in which one can be, in the best sense, self-focused. For some participants, it is the first time in many years, if at all, that they have been away *alone*. Aside from the particular didactic content of the Institute, this aspect in itself is quite powerful. One participant in my small group, for example, wrote to me in the fall that she had gone back home having decided that she would marry the man she had been dating, a hard decision after a first marriage that had ended in divorce. I had known nothing of this personal and private portion of her agenda for her week's sojourn. For those teachers who experience their week with us as a retreat, it is not uncommon for the Institute to be an opportunity for self-evaluation, for psychologically taking control of one's life course.

To be away from one's usual setting is to be removed not only from responsibilities but also from one's supports and structures, from ways in which one usually exists in one's various roles unself-consciously (that is, without self-consciousness in either of its two meanings: self-awareness or embarrassed self-observation). As in a saying variously attributed to Sigmund Freud and a Zen monk, "The fish is the last to discover the water," existential questions do not rise easily to the fore when one is embedded in one's daily environment. Being removed from this embeddedness at the institute presents an opportunity for awareness of choice in one's life, a prospect which may be exciting and/or frightening. Whether one returns to one's usual settings with new plans or with self-renewed commitment to old paths, one's environment, both professional and personal, can be seen more *in relief* because it can be seen in contrast.

The word "retreat" calls forth feelings of peacefulness and solitude, conditions that (in candor) may be more wished for than realized at the Institutes. We offer participants the opportunity to be students, to be relieved of incessant faculty responsibilities for *providing*. But there are stresses, too. Just as we sometimes delightfully fantasize being a child again, we realize that such an opportunity would not be a state of unalloyed joy and ease. And so it is at the Institute when teachers become students once again. It is anxiety-producing to meet many new people (including, sometimes, one's self), to measure one's own performance against that of others and, more importantly, against one's own ideals, and to face (or face not facing) feelings engendered by a role play or a co-participant's personal revelation. Our task as faculty is to keep this anxiety within the range that is optimal for learning—to be aroused, but not terrified. We try to maintain this balance in many ways, one of which is our attention to mealtimes. By serving excellent food, with amenities of ambience and service, we hope to provide a centering place for the participants and for us to relax and share experiences, both personal and professional. Newly developing bonds of friendship help to create a safe emotional environment in which to be one's self and to take risks.

We offer the participants three types of learning experiences—experiential, didactic, and modeling. We not only provide opportunities for learners who differ in preferred methods of processing material, we also reinforce learning because of multiple presentations in various modes that work synergistically.

Because the most important aspects of effective counseling are already nascent within the counselor's experience, the importance of the didactic presentations (the Institute lectures) is not primarily in the presentation of new material but in supplying cognitive frameworks for the organization of that experience. Not only have a significant number of the participants taken courses or read about adolescence, but most have known more developing adolescents in the classroom than the Institute faculty has known in the consulting room. One of the most pleasing responses to our lectures for me is some variant of, "That's it! That just describes my experience, but I didn't know what I knew."

The lectures, of which there are about a dozen, address content areas: counseling, normal development, symptomatic problems, and boundaries of appropriate counseling areas for teachers. The most variable in content over the years have been those dealing with symptomatic problems. Eating disorders, for example, are a marked worry for teachers now. Substance abuse is again an area of great concern and has been reinserted in the formal program after an absence of several years. In part, this variation is a response to the fact that teachers are being confronted with frightening and life-threatening disturbances. However, the changing lecture topics reflect not so much changes in what most students are concerned with most of the time (relationships, self-esteem, independence) as changes in what we adults feel most anxious about, what we feel least equipped to deal with. Over the years, for example, there has appeared, disappeared, and reappeared a specific lecture on sexuality.

This phenomenon reflected a shift in mores that made many teachers feel more able to discuss students' sexual lives without being "blown out of the water." Now, of course, there is the new concern with sexuality prompted by the specter of AIDS.

The didactic lectures not only organize experience but provide a cognitive framework in which to manage the teacher-counselor's anxiety. For example, "Red Flags," the lecture on recognizing, evaluating, and coping with emergencies or situations in which one should obtain outside help, is a spur to rehearse the handling of possible future crises. It also provides a memory to be called upon in such a crisis—the lecturer's voice or words or concepts as an accompanying internal guide—when one may feel suddenly panicked and alone.

Throughout the institutes there are opportunities for learning by observing faculty, each of whom is an experienced psychotherapist, in formal and informal demonstrations of counseling. Studies on effectiveness of psychotherapy show that more experienced therapists are more effective than those with less experience. And modeling, learning from others' performance of a task, is one of the ways that people learn. At least twice during the Institute, the faculty presents formal role plays, followed by discussion with participants. We may present a situation, for example, of a worried or depressed student asking to speak to a teacher, or of an angry student called in by the dean for a serious disciplinary violation. We may start with a situation in which it may be more or less apparent from the beginning of the encounter that a counseling stance is appropriate, then go to one with an initially willing or unwilling counselee or any of the other myriad situations in which students present themselves to a teacher or administrator. Each role play is unrehearsed and is usually planned only to the extent of outlining the presenting situation.

At its most effective, the role play presents not perfection but, rather, the reality of the counseling situation in which a real human (imperfect) counselor can help a student come to know and esteem himself better. The counseling role play that looks *too* smooth, where the counselor steps deftly from rock to rock through the torrent of the student's spoken or unspoken feeling—rage, sorrow, silent withdrawal, contempt, shame—without even getting his shoes wet, tends to be good theater but is likely to lead to withdrawal by the participants. They often say, "I could *never* do that," or, perhaps in defense against feelings of lowered self-esteem, "That's an unrealistic situation; no student would behave like that." There have been a few times, indeed, when we have engineered a poor beginning to show the ways in which a bad initial encounter can be turned around. But role playing the cloud that has a silver lining is usually quite unintended. Our imperfections are real and the mistakes that the participants point out are often truly just that.

There have been at least three formal role plays per institute among five to seven faculty members over 25 years, as well as countless informal ones in the small groups. The sometimes surprising pleasure for us is that they always seem alive, although the scenarios come to have similarities over time, as do the players. Preston Munter speaks of the person in the teacher in the counselor meeting the person in the student in the counselee. In each role play, regardless of the stated scenario, we inevitably play some part of ourselves, while, at the same time, there is an opportunity for us to play and encounter each other (and ourselves) in different aspects. Different "persons in the counselor" show the participants the varied counseling styles of experienced senior clinicians, each of which can be effective. Our similarities in philosophy, our agreement with Jane Levy's definition of counseling as a process of fostering understanding and growth through a relationship of empathic listening and clarification of feelings, is expressed through our own personalities. And within each individual personality, each of us also differs in interactions with different "persons in the counselee" as a reflection of empathic attunement. Thus, although I generally may be more talkative than some colleagues and more likely to use humor, I will be much quieter with a depressed counselee than an angry one. My knowledge and acceptance of my own style in the counseling situation helps me to monitor and control my own behavior—to talk less, for example—without sacrificing my genuineness, my sense of being myself.

Every counseling situation, whether in a role play or in real life, will differ with the participants (and their past experiences, present concerns, future plans), with the setting (and its constraints and supports), and with the problem (and its meanings to each). Thus, we cannot and do not wish to model, "Here's how to handle a depressed student or a rule-breaking student or an anorexic student," based on the problem and not the person. We hope to present an attitude about the importance and values of counseling in which we truly believe, the skills that serve the process, and the commitment to the self-exploration in our counselees and in ourselves that keeps us learning.

We cannot expect participants to be non-judgmental with counselees if we take a judgmental stance towards them and what they are
open enough to share. Any institute or institution is, in certain respects, like a family, with the faculty or administration setting unspoken norms of expected behavior. Often, for example, a rise in
acting out and friction within a student body is an unconscious communication about faculty conflict. To make our week-long "home"
safe for exploration, we as faculty must attend to our own relationships. As in our formal role plays, we cannot present a model of perfection. We strive to present a model of our struggles with our
imperfections.

A few years ago, for example, one faculty member role-played the
teacher of another who played a student upset about his grade on a
paper. The role play went poorly. The teacher-counselor seemed to
need an admission from the student that the paper was indeed bad
before he would explore the feelings that the student was expressing
in garbled fashion through the content of the paper. The student became more distressed and frustrated, but because there was underlying affection between the role players, as there often is between the
counselor and counselee, the student kept his composure. The role
play finally ended, though not in a crescendo of good feeling. Watching it was painful and also quite confusing. Afterward, the faculty
member who had been playing the teacher came to the realization
that he had arrived at the institute feeling upset over the mistreat-
ment of a friend by someone who he felt would not take responsibility
for his actions. This was the emotional link that, in the role play, had
kept him prodding the student to admit that he had done poorly on
the paper and should have taken responsibility for it despite his
feelings.

In a subsequent role play at his own suggestion, the two faculty
members played out the pair's next meeting. Without burdening the
student with all of the details, he acknowledged that his own feelings
of anger over an unrelated situation had prevented him from really
listening to the student. This straightforward admission helped them
get their relationship back on track. Thus, the faculty member modeled for the institute participants as well as for the student in the role
play the interference of the teacher's unacknowledged feelings with
his functioning as a counselor and the growth that both teacher and
student found in self-exploration.

All learning must at some level be experiential to be integrated into oneself. Sometimes that experiencing is in memory, in fantasy, or in silent rehearsal. If the listener to my lecture on adolescence, for example, gives no thought to her own or her students' or her child's adolescence, she is not really hearing me. But, experiential learning also has a specific meaning in our presenting the participants with opportunities for self-exploration and practice in skill-building.

The small groups, which meet at least once and sometimes twice each day for one and a half to two hours, are multipurpose. It is here that the major portion of the work of the institute is done. The groups are task-centered in that they are oriented toward talking about students and role playing counseling situations. Though open to the self-exploration that is so essential to the effective use of the self as a counselor, they are not therapy or encounter groups which have self-revelation as the primary aim. Such personal sharing does indeed occur and is welcome, but it usually happens as one is coming to understand what is interfering with the counseling process.

Central to this experiential learning is the role play, a powerful, multifaceted learning opportunity. Role playing has roots in the "let's pretend" of childhood ("You be the daddy and I'll be the mommy"). It is a potentially rich experience for participants and observers alike. The most useful response to, "What should you do (or what do you do in your school) about kids who hang around you all the time, or kids who don't want to be counseled, or who take drugs?" is something like, "Is there someone you have in mind?" Abstract discussion of issues is often a way all of us use to defend against our anxieties about our competence, our vulnerability, and our fears of intimacy with our students or fellow group members. Whether having just completed the school year at the Northfield Institute or about to start a new one at the Fountain Valley Institute, the participants have particular students on their minds. And particular students usually stay on our minds because we have doubts about our relationship to them; something has not worked in our attempts to help them.

Often in a role play, the participant who is concerned about how to counsel a particular student plays that student, whom he can usually portray better than a participant unfamiliar with that student. It is likely to be a revelatory experience. It certainly enhances empathy to walk in someone else's moccasins, even if only in fantasy play. In trying to see the situation through the student's eyes, one often understands much more of the complexity of the student's dilemma, the meaning of his actions to him, and how the interventions of the teacher-counselor might feel to the student. A more empathic and effective plan of response usually appears rather naturally, leading to renewed hope which will allow the teacher to try again to relate to, rather than to abandon and isolate, the troubled and troubling student.

The role plays enhance empathy not only for the students but for each other and for ourselves. From the audience, it is much easier to be sure of how to do it right, and it is often humbling to step in for a counselor who is stuck only to get stuck oneself just a little further down the line. Role-play counselees can provide explicit verbal feedback about how the counselor's responses feel to the student and what was facilitating about what the role-play counselor said or did. More than that, role-play students can often specify what could have been more helpful in a way that real-life counselees rarely do, permitting quicker self-correction for the role-play counselor. Often one learns from such feedback that the responses assumed to be most effective are considerably less than that. For example, an attempt to help a student progress faster by suggesting problem-solving tactics, though well meant, can reveal a failure of empathy—a failure to accept who and where the student is at that moment.

As mentioned previously, we always role play ourselves in some part. And this, too, is often a path to self-knowledge, whether one plays student or teacher. For example, I once role played a boarding school student who was very depressed because she had gotten a *B* on a French exam. In the role play, I was a scholarship student who had never gotten less than an *A* and who felt that my ability to get top grades was the only thing I had going for me to get into a prestigious college and from there into medical school. Frightened that this *B* meant that I couldn't do the work, and lost without my Plan, I was panicky and depressed. The role play ended with my feeling somewhat calmer and hopeful enough to be willing to talk again with the counselor, but *my* mood remained stuck in the role play. I had not been in any obvious way like the student I played, and, my concerns about returning to work after my maternity leave were worlds away from those of the girl I played. I recognized, however, that in playing this girl, I was obsessed with her dilemma—responding with humor and stuck in a mindset she knew was limiting. In short, I was playing myself. I had to look at my own current internal stress, realizing that I was more in distress (and defending against it) about my going back to work than I had acknowledged.

Role playing, interestingly, is also a way to foster attitude change, for research[3] has shown that people's attitudes tend to move in the direction of those values that they express in the role play. In teaching counseling, there are attitudes that we wish to enhance, and role playing a warm, genuine, empathic, non-punitive, non-controlling, non-action-oriented counselor is likely to increase such behavior in real life.

In a way, the small group is a role play in itself in that in a certain sense it casts each participant in the role of counselee. In attending to one's own feelings and one's own growth, one grapples with—and hopefully has more sympathy for—the feelings that make the counselee want to hide from himself and from the counselor, as well as the hope, bravery, and wish for a relationship that allows him to go forward and reveal himself.

In providing an environment that fosters the participants' growth as individuals and as counselors, we value the same attitudes that foster growth in counselees. We feel true warm regard and respect for these teachers, intelligent and committed to their profession. We try to be ourselves with them and to understand and prize their struggles with the new role of counselor. Aside from the feedback they get from their role-play counselees, we do not evaluate the participants' performance (although they evaluate all aspects of our program in "reactionaires"). Building trust and structuring an environment where people can take chances, explore themselves, and try out new skills is our main task, and to do this rather quickly requires care and attention. Whatever benefits might accrue from evaluating participants' performance and suggesting better interventions would come at high cost, indeed, and would also counter our belief that the relationship, not the technique, is the healing element.

Schools Teaching Counseling to Teachers

The program as we have designed it at Northfield and Fountain Valley suits us. As I suggested, it has its own constraints in being a one-shot, once-in-a-lifetime introduction to counseling. (Participants can attend only once.) Providing education and support for teachers who

---

[3]Alan C. Elms (Ed.), *Role Playing, Reward, and Attitude Change* (New York: Van Nostrand Reinhold Company, 1969).

counsel students in schools requires some of the elements that we provide in our institute programs and some that we do not.

Counseling takes place within a relationship, and the teacher-student relationship exists within a network of other relationships with students, teachers, peers, administrators, trustees, and parents. Counseling involves feelings both for the student and the teacher. It must not be a solitary endeavor. Before even beginning to teach counseling to teachers, two questions must be addressed: Does the school support teachers counseling students, and do the teachers want to do it? We take a firm position that a teacher who does not wish to counsel students for any reason—she doesn't believe in it, he doesn't think he has the talent, she's feeling too bound up with family problems to wish to hear students'—should not do so. A relationship that rests on concern and genuineness is distorted if the teacher feels coerced. And if the teacher feels that the administration will not support her in being open to hear whatever the student brings, she cannot provide the necessary conditions of safety.

Teaching beginning teacher-counselors and supporting their work requires three elements: a didactic component, an experiential component, and a relationship component. The teacher needs to know what counseling is, how it differs from other roles played with students. The teacher needs to learn about crises, emergencies, and other situations where help is needed, and how to go about getting that help: how to make a referral, how to set up an emergency plan, how to inquire about suicidal behavior. The teacher should have some framework for understanding normal adolescent development and the "normative crises" and issues of those years for both boys and girls. Learning about more serious dysfunctions such as anorexia or depression or psychosis should not be seen as preparation to be a counselor for students with these disorders; rather, its purpose is to enable one to recognize them, to seek appropriate help, and to provide support to the student if he remains in the school.

Role playing is clearly the best tool for learning and practicing counseling skills. It provides a safe place to practice, a way of getting immediate feedback, and a new path to seeing situations from the students' perspective. It is the backbone of any program teaching counselors. It does not have to be monitored or evaluated by a professional counselor or therapist. A group of peers can be an excellent setting for role play and discussion.

The group of peers, with or without the participation of a consultant, is essential not only to learning counseling but also to continuing counseling as well. A group of teachers who meet regularly offer each to the other a necessary place to share concerns about students, about one's own counseling interactions, about one's own feelings.

How these elements are arranged will differ from school to school, depending on the needs and resources of each. In distinction to hiring trained counselors who have obtained education on their own, teaching counseling to teachers is a responsibility of the school. Some have sent teachers to institutes such as Northfield or Fountain Valley; some have workshops within the school, with outside professionals brought in; some hire a consultant to work within the school over time to teach and supervise counseling work by teachers. Teachers should not be expected (or allowed) to counsel students without some formal introduction to counseling and ongoing support.

Teachers who are experienced with adolescents, who have good relationships with students, and who have developed the interpersonal skills that are most helpful in counseling are an enormous resource in providing counseling in schools. To support teachers in this endeavor enriches their experience, opening new realms of relationships with the students. For students, especially those who will not need or seek the services of a psychotherapist, these teachers trained in listening skills can provide an experience of self-exploration in a relationship with a caring adult that often reverberates long after and far beyond the often brief encounter.

Chapter 6

THE CLIMATE OF THE SCHOOL

Preston K. Munter

Whether counseling is accepted and effective in a school depends on a number of factors which, for our purposes, we think of as comprising the major components of the culture or climate of the school. That is true in any school, whether the counseling is such as we espouse at the Northfield-Fountain Valley Counseling Institutes or any other. In a sense, the effectiveness of any counseling program is a good deal more dependent on the nature of the school's climate than it is on the technical expertise of the teachers who do the counseling, or on the particular nature of the counseling program, or even on the style of individual counselors. In this chapter, then, we will consider some of the important—even essential—elements which make for the sort of school climate conducive to effective counseling relationships.

Basic Elements of Climate

Overall there are two basic aspects of the climate of any school which become essential ingredients of a counseling program and which can have a critical impact on it. First is the tradition of the school. If it encompasses a genuine concern for the well-being of students beyond their intellectual competence, a counseling program could flourish there. Hopefully, such a tradition would honor the view that education is only a part—however major—of the long-term and fundamental process of students' growth, without foregoing the responsibility

101

of helping them develop skills in short-term academic tasks such as reading and writing. The aphorism of Colonel Parker in Chicago, "Tame 'em, train 'em, teach 'em," was an effective, if somewhat simplistic, educational philosophy that might prove nurturant even now in the practice of a counseling approach. It would be especially effective in tandem with another faculty tendency which may appear to be somewhat paradoxical, even if only on the surface: The *instinct* on the part of the faculty and administration to be reasonably flexible and compassionate in dealing with individual students—that is, not worrying too obsessively about "consistency" from one student to another.

It is extremely difficult, perhaps impossible, to achieve consistency in dealing with adolescents. In a way, consistency becomes invalidated by the natural and undeniable individuation among students. "Inconsistent!" is a cry heard from parents and students in reaction to school experiences they either do not understand at all or interpret in rather parochial, even narcissistic terms—especially when they feel inclined to discuss a given situation "in general" from "an educational point of view." However, *not* being treated as individuals—that is, being treated *consistently*—is likely to prompt an even louder cry of pain from students in academic trouble.

Accordingly, while we certainly support the notion of fairness and equity in disciplinary matters, we also urge that the granting of rewards and the imposition of limitations and punishments in disciplinary matters be realistically grounded in each case. Only in this way can the school deal with students having problems on a case-by-case basis in a sufficiently flexible manner but within an understood set of values and standards. A counseling approach provides the most effective resolution to this perennial dilemma in school. Even so, how to apply the rules and how to set conditions equitably when individual life situations vary so widely and painful remains essentially irresolvable in any neat and tidy way.

The second basic ingredient of a school climate if it is to be nurturant to counseling is the authenticity of the principle of confidentiality. Trust in the privacy of communication which is clearly designated as such—which it should be—is an *absolute*, essential and compelling reality in a school if counseling is to take hold. Students and teachers with any degree of self-respect and honest commitment will not—cannot—allow themselves to express the very things that are crucial to the process of resolving problems if they fear that their confidence is not being honored. The relationships among faculty, administration, and students must allow confidentiality of communication and support it honestly, fully, and faithfully. It is not too much to say that without that basic tenet built into the culture of the school, no counseling program of any value to students or of worth to the educational program of the school can possibly succeed.

But it should be clear that the principle and practice of confidentiality does not mean that there can be *no* communication about personal matters within the school community. What it does mean is that communication which is designated as confidential must be held that way, unless it is agreed between the parties concerned (as more often than not it can be) to transmit certain parts of it to appropriately concerned others such as parents and other counselors. Indeed, in this sense, beyond a protection of the privacy of individuals, confidentiality provides a sensitive context in which necessary messages and information can be shared with those who may have an important or special need to know in order to play their role in whatever means are being undertaken to help students resolve their problems.

Like everything else in life except birth and death, of course, confidentiality is not an absolute. Protecting the life of an individual or the integrity of the school community must take precedence over the privacy of communication when such risks are clear and present. But in the absence of these risks, communication between counselor and student must be sacrosanct. If that aspect of the climate of the school falls into question, the fundamental purpose of a counseling program becomes vitiated and can only proceed on a pro forma, hypocritical basis in which students will rightly restrain themselves from sharing the very information about their feelings that is the main business of counseling.

Of course there are many difficulties associated with maintaining privacy of communication in the context of everyday realities in any school situation. Realistically, then, the teacher's job is to communicate with students so that they are able to use what is inside where their strengths are to cope with what is outside where the challenges are. In other words, the internal process is there anyway: Students have personal and sensitive concerns, and teachers hear about them unavoidably in one way or another. At some level or other, teachers deal with the internal process in the student, with their feelings and relationships in the ordinary course of events. At first glance, these matters may seem to be in opposition to one another. Thought and feeling, after all, stand in an organic, dynamic interaction with each other. So there is actually no way for a teacher *not* to deal with them simultaneously, whether or not the teacher sees himself or herself as a counselor. As Janet Sand says elsewhere in this volume, the feelings are there in any case. So there is really no choice for teachers except that of being sensitive and accepting about what they hear from students and listening for it. In performing this double task—these two aspects of which are only apparently at odds—the teacher must have an integral sense of himself or herself.

Another way of looking at this somewhat paradoxical situation is that growth is to some extent an adversary process in which students are in full flight, in the full panoply of their rebellion, and at the peak of their anxiety about adulthood. They are plagued by painful ambivalences toward themselves and adults about dependency, autonomy, and competence, and at the same time they are hungry for a positive sense of self-esteem. Can they be loving and lovable people? These are intense feelings and personal needs which make students at once vulnerable and provocative. If teachers are to be effective advisers when confronted with such ambiguity and paradox, they must be able to deal with their own personal and professional needs and must be capable of fulfilling them in appropriate ways—that is to say in ways that extend their own growth by satisfying their adult needs in peer relationships. Like students, teachers need to develop the capacity to tolerate disappointment, loss or release of control, challenges to their values, and simultaneous devaluation and praise. As the target of intense feelings, they must deal with closeness and distance in interpersonal relationships and the most difficult loss of all—the reality of gradually being displaced, of becoming unnecessary, in their students' lives. In summary, teachers must learn to be and to become worthy adversaries in their students' struggle to grow. Both teacher and student have to live with anger, loss, and anxiety while they search for bonding and love. Even teachers need to be cared about, because caretakers need to be cared for like everyone else.

Maintaining the Right Teacher/Student Relationship

In order to help create an appropriate climate in their schools, teachers must sustain their own self-esteem. Meeting this acute need is a

difficult task in a social system that demands much of teachers but rewards them with comparatively little—much less, in fact, than it rewards people in other professions which require less training,
discipline, and responsibility. Furthermore, the academic setting
emphasizes, as perhaps no other, the reality of the life cycle. The
commitment to teaching narrows the reality options of teachers and
makes the cost of some losses very high. Therefore, a strong sense of
self is a prime need. But self-esteem comes from inside, especially
from relationships with colleagues and from a strong awareness of
and sensitivity to themselves. And they must develop this awareness
without being smug, parochial, or defensive or becoming trapped in
a private sense of having *the* universal insight or truth. All of these
pitfalls are difficult to avoid. Ultimately self-esteem can come only
from a realistic sense of self-fulfillment in ongoing ways, as a continuing possibility in a general sense as well as actually in particular
circumstances.

A special quality of self-consciousness on the part of teacher-counselors is therefore a necessity. They need to be mindful, for example,
of the risks inherent in vicariously living out their lives in those of
their students and of the danger in being cast *in loco parentis*. This
is a troublesome concept at best and one which is intrinsically unrealistic with respect to students' feelings toward their parents versus those toward their teachers. Teacher-counselors need to resolve
their own personal confusions and dilemmas, so that they do not become vulnerable to those beguiling but unrealistically misplaced
feelings students sometimes project onto them. They must also be
careful not to inject such feelings in the form of inappropriate value
judgments into their teaching or counseling. In short, they need to
face the enemy inside themselves so that they do not over-identify
with students. They must always be alert to their natural desire and
legitimate need to develop healthy relationships with students while
remaining adult role models with their own perspective and for their
own purposes and growth, separate and apart from the needs of their
students. The school has both a moral and educational obligation to
support them in this objective. Nothing makes a school climate
healthier than interpersonal relationships between teachers and students which clarify the distinctiveness of their roles, but this differentiation certainly does not mean standing at a distance from
students or being afraid to be close to them.

From another perspective, mutuality in teacher-student relationships substantially contributes to a healthy school climate. Being an adult role model means monitoring and making use of the clear and real differences in attitudes, maturity, experience, and—above all— wisdom, between teachers and their students. The validity and utility of their relationships with students lie in the exchange of values and feelings between them and in having the courage and didactic sensitivity to exploit the opportunities that appear serendipitously in the course of their work together and to engage in dialogue about such matters. That dialogue—sometimes called counseling—is what supports growth in students and provides special satisfaction to teachers.

A Question of Needs

We have referred to mutuality in the teacher-counselor-student relationship as an important element in the climate of the school. To a large extent, the presence or absence of that mutuality is determined by how teachers play out their own needs. The way they express certain specific needs, for example, can seriously affect the climate of the school. Among those needs which can be especially detrimental to the support a school climate must give to counselors are (1) the need to be liked, (2) the need to know everything, and (3) the need to "rescue" students who are in trouble.

The need to be liked can be seen as a residual problem of most adults, probably an outcome of concern about parental caring in their own developmental years. That is to say, it is a form of expressing their own unresolved losses and, as such, is a narcissistic defense against the fear of not being liked and a need to compensate for those early losses, real or fantasied as they may be. But teaching is a test of personality as well as of mind, and teachers must relate well to their students. That does not necessarily mean being liked by students as much as it means being respected by them for supporting their growth. If the teachers' own needs to be liked are too strong a determinant, they will create distance in their relationships with students by shifting the necessary counseling focus from their students to themselves. That shift beclouds the growth-inducing climate that should exist in a school. An excessive need to be liked on the part of the teacher-counselor, as opposed to *liking* to be liked—a perfectly healthy state—is destructive to student-teacher relationships. That is true not only in the context of counseling but generally in the class-room and otherwise in the school because it serves the teacher, not the student. In doing so, *needing* to be liked interferes with the positive impact teachers can have as adult role models. Teachers who want to be liked by their students *too much* place at risk the mutual respect they can readily earn by taking the necessary risks that all useful and positive human encounters entail.

In the same vein, it is important for teachers not to imitate students on the mistaken grounds that to be *like* them is to be *liked* by them. Teachers who ape students in attitudes, language, and behavior, to say nothing of dress, create a threatening climate in a school. At bottom, teachers have only adulthood to offer students. To abandon that in favor of what can only be described as empty and inappropriate imitation devalues adulthood, thereby confusing students by eradicating the clear differences between teachers and students which they need in the adversary process of growth. Teachers thus need to set limits for students, whether students seem to like them for doing so or not; they should not try to control students but help them in the natural developmental process of integrating control of themselves.

Adolescents are, indeed, likely to become frightened in the absence of reasonable limits: They grow and mature with appropriate limit-setting because it facilitates the natural developmental processes by which they internalize their capacity to be their own authority. Students like teachers best when teachers like themselves sufficiently that they do not *need* to be liked as a prerequisite to being helpful. Teachers can enjoy being liked by their students when they have earned it by helping them grow. Life is, after all, a circular pattern, not a linear one. Dostoevsky lurks around every corner, ready to make those inescapable and fateful connections.

The need to be omniscient, to know all or, at least, a good deal, and to have special knowledge and insights so that one is perceived by students as being powerful is seductive. It is also somewhat delusional. The attitude, "What I know is the truth," for example, suggests that the teacher considers his or her control best and most effective. This attitude may be a reaction by teachers to anxiety of their own which, developmentally, relates to an unconscious fear of loss of self-control. In any case, this authoritarian stance has a negative impact on the climate of the school. It is likely to shut out the sources of information of most use to teacher-counselors in understanding their students and, at the same time, of most use to students. The latter must have access to their own experience, both internal and external, if they are to work through their own problems.

If teachers' knowledge is to be of positive use to their students, it must be communicated in a compassionate sharing of their own inner experience, person to person. Such sharing is the best preventive against any sort of omnipotent control. It helps avoid the anxiety that leads to premature intellectual closure on the part of students. It also helps teachers *listen* so they can *hear* the *other* human experience that is *always* and *inevitably* different. When that is a hallmark of a school's climate, healthy growth can proceed for teacher and student alike.

The so-called rescue fantasy, probably an expression of the teacher's own fear of being lost or abandoned and the need to be rescued, is all too commonplace among teachers. As such, it plays a significant part in the nature of the climate of a school.

Essentially, the rescue fantasy is a distorted notion that if students come to a teacher for help, it must be because of the teacher's special capacities—or even powers. These teachers come to believe that they are omniscient and that they are obligated to solve whatever problems students bring to them. Teachers must be careful not to be seduced into the beguiling belief that they have unique understanding and insights and that the obvious affection and esteem in which students hold them will enable them to snatch them from the depths of their despair and trouble, even though parents, physicians, ministers, friends, therapists, and previous teacher-counselors were unable to accomplish that very thing. It is worth remembering that anyone who is extremely difficult to "straighten out" probably has the capacity to outwit or otherwise sabotage even the most skillful, highly motivated, and best-intentioned "helper."

Teachers beset by the rescue fantasy are tempted to *do* something *to* their students rather than work *with* them to help them mobilize their own resources—that is, to rescue rather than facilitate for their own reasons rather than those of their students, toward their own goals rather than those of their students. Rescuers tell their students in what way and how to correct what is wrong; they give them advice, a notably ineffective method of bringing about change in people. By so doing, they rearrange reality, no doubt out of compassion for their troubled students. Their hope and intention is to make the environment "therapeutic" so that the qualities the rescuing teacher "knows" the student possesses can be mobilized and made applicable. This process leaves students with a clear sense of their own incompetence, a realistic response to a school climate which not only allows but encourages students not to take risks in their own behalf. At the same time, it allows and encourages teacher-counselors to take over the resolution of their students' problems rather than helping them understand the school and its resources—and even the teacher-counselor—sufficiently well to act wisely in their own behalf. The struggle toward independence is a truly growth-inducing process to which students have a right and which is essential to the long-term purposes of their education. In this, the climate of the school plays an instrumental and unavoidable role.

Faculty/Administration Interaction

The last factor we shall consider in establishing an appropriate counseling climate in a school is the quality of interaction among faculty and administration. Insofar as counseling is concerned—to say nothing of the overall quality of life in a school generally—this interaction is an important aspect of the climate of a school because of the actual and potential extent to which it affects every aspect of life there. Indeed, it is the clearest direct expression of the quality of life in a school. Like the relationship between a husband and wife and its effects on the life of their family, the quality of faculty and administrative interpersonal relationships critically govern the style and degree of humaneness which characterizes most relationships in a school. In that sense, the interaction among faculty makes effective counseling possible or impossible. Accordingly it is worth our while to discuss in some detail the basic elements which make for healthy faculty interaction.

As a first step, faculty must be temperamentally as well as intellectually disposed to care for and about one another. Ideally this should be a spontaneous response within the faculty. But if it does not happen spontaneously, then cognitive recognition of that need can serve as a basis for developing faculty relationships. Ultimately a reasonable degree of community caretaking emerges. Such caring and the compassion it stimulates drives out the fear and anxiety that so frequently characterize groups of people like teachers who feel undervalued and who are bound in other ways by common anxieties, interests, skills, goals, and realities. Furthermore, this interaction is the basis of the trust among faculty that is utterly essential to healthy interacting at all levels—personal, social, and professional. Most importantly, it is a wellspring of self-esteem in a profession not overly endowed with such a resource and lacking ready access to ample reservoirs of it.

Linked closely with caring and trust, confidentiality is of central importance to healthy faculty relationships. Faculty must accord themselves the privilege of confidential communications, not just those essential to counseling dialogues but also formal and informal communications. The sanctity of privacy, in short, is a key ingredient of strong and productive faculty-to-faculty relationships. While this premise is especially applicable to the faculty of boarding schools, it is unimaginable that any faculty in any school can function effectively as teachers or with peers and colleagues unless they trust each other sufficiently to protect the element of privacy in their communications with each other. Privacy makes their workplace safe enough so that they as well as their students can test themselves and can, in fact, take the personal, intellectual, and emotional risks that are the precursors of healthy growth within any faculty group.

Thus, caring, trust, and authentic privacy form a background against which it becomes possible for a faculty to present itself as appropriate and realistic role models to its students—in other words, as having the courage to be themselves. Without deserting or camouflaging their personal authenticity, they can model, as well, the teacher as counselor and the counselor as teacher, the linkage being their common responsibilities, goals, and interests and feelings. It then becomes possible, also, to take the sometimes painful risks entailed in struggling to cope with closeness and intimacy versus distance in relationships with each other as well as in encounters with students. Those struggles are a seminal dynamic in a school in the continuing growth process of adults as well as that of adolescents. Reflexive and honest interaction among faculty is highly dependent upon both the process and outcome of that kind of personal confrontation, and it requires realization by faculty that their interactions and interpersonal relationships are protected by a shared sensitivity to their mutually acknowledged and respected vulnerabilities.

The Faculty Team

The fundamental triadic functions of the faculty team are those of teacher, counselor, and administrator. The validity of their teamship, aside from whatever personal and serendipitous bonding is involved, lies in the educational experiences and responsibilities shared; the basic concepts of education and its proper goals; the quality of relationships modeled; and the varying teaching styles and the values they propound, demonstrate, and live, both as individuals and corporately.

At the same time—and despite the implied and actual commonalities already indicated—the strength of a faculty team is also very much derived from an adherence to their role differentiations to whatever degree they may find possible and realistic. The counseling and disciplinary functions, for example, should not be carried out by the same person if at all possible. By the same token, a faculty member should wear as few hats as possible rather than—as is too often the case—as many as can be imposed. The bureaucratic responsibilities of faculty outside the classroom erode their time for informal and person-to-person relationships with each other, no less than with students, and they should be kept to the essential minimum.

Personal success is defined by the school community and by the larger community around it. It is important for faculty, however, to resist as far as possible the blandishments of "success," elusive as they are in the stereotypic sense of money, position, and power. The latter serve to displace the more durable values of solid investments in their own interrelationships from which they so largely draw the intellectual and emotional resources that produce some of the more profound satisfactions of teaching.

In no sense, however, do I suggest that faculty should not have concerns about adequate compensation or that their commitment to teaching should disenfranchise them from their just, honest, and realistic material and monetary needs. In the course of filling their understandable need to explore their own individual potential for success, measured by whatever criteria, teachers need to be mindful of differentiating the rather immature *need* for success from a healthy capacity to enjoy success when they have earned it. In that connection, faculty must stand ready to offer a compassionate sharing with one another of the losses imposed on all of them by the relentless realities of the life cycle. There is a reinforcing interplay between those and the patterned, predictable, repetitive, and *multiple* losses inherent in academic life. As generations of students come and go, they take with them the heavy personal investments teachers make in them, leaving teachers with the inescapable experience of being displaced, of having become unnecessary in their students' lives, especially in the lives they honestly and appropriately care about. Like no other profession, teaching imposes on its practitioners the unavoidable necessity of coping with a chronic sense of loss. This comes to be more and more psychologically costly as teachers progress through the life cycle with its own inevitable losses. At the same time, faculties in which the impact of these losses can be shared offer their members a kind of support that can be remarkably healing and sustaining. The ripple effect of that sharing on the entire climate of the school and on all of the relationships which so intimately occupy everyone in it has a unique force in enhancing the self-esteem of the faculty.

Effective communication among faculty members plays a special role in the quality of faculty interaction and, therefore, of the climate of the school. How effective it can be is chiefly determined by how openly teachers can engage with each other while paying due respect to the sanctity of individual confidences. In practice, this engagement may be a sensitive and somewhat risky matter in some schools where, sadly, teachers are mistrustful of one another, especially of the maverick who marches to a different drum. Mistrust among teachers about educational matters, such as process versus substance in the classroom, and differences of view about affective and cognitive learning can close off communication. Discussion about those very issues, among the most basic in education, should serve to stimulate and reinforce open communication within the faculty. In short, while there may be potential conflict within a faculty over differing orientations toward basic educational issues, processes, and systems, in a healthy faculty those same differences become the theme of truly productive communication. As such they elaborate the growth-inducing factors which impact so directly and positively on the school climate. Effective and open communication among faculty makes for such a positive overall experience for students that it is unmistakable, and its educational value is unarguable.

The nurturance of difference among faculty as well as among students not only strengthens the quality of faculty interaction but is, at the same time, a way of demonstrating what that quality is operationally. A diverse faculty is a notably effective educational instrument. Varying cognitive and personality styles stimulate creative thinking in students. A wide range of attitudes and values helps students to grow emotionally and to explore the reach of their talents and curiosity. Beyond making it possible for students to enrich their educational experience, teachers can potentiate their own personal and professional growth. So doing helps prevent them from feeling estranged from their colleagues and depersonalized by academic routine and its accompanying bureaucratic demands. More importantly, open and candid communication among faculty helps them integrate the many losses of their own academic and personal lives which are, in any case, unavoidable.

This environment becomes possible because full and open communication can take place among faculty members with an especially low level of risk. There are few other places in our society where people who work closely together toward common basic goals and objectives are better able to tolerate the defenses that define their separate experiences and lifestyles. At the same time, they need the capacity and willingness to share those differences and to confront those vulnerabilities and individual experiences, however different, which can have so significant and useful an impact on the entire faculty. When that occurs, the quality of life for everyone at a school becomes stimulating, exciting, and uniquely exhilarating.

Setting Appropriate Limits

Finally, healthy faculty interaction can come about only if there is a disposition among its members to establish and maintain appropriate limit-setting in the school. This applies to faculty and administrators themselves no less than to students. For a long time faculties have fallen into, have been led into, or have allowed themselves to be seduced into taking on too much responsibility. As a result, their lives—personal and professional, alike—have become pressured to the point of being overstressed. The consequent effect on the quality of school life is altogether negative. Faculties, therefore, must stand their ground against the excessive demands of parents and of administrators who bend to such demands. There is a certain relaxed quality inherent in the very nature of academic life that is essential to intellectual pursuits. Faculty therefore must have the disposition, the courage, and the strength to fight, if need be, for this condition against oppositional forces that exist in and around a school deeply resourced with money, power, and influence. It is no service to a school community or to parents—and certainly not to students—for faculties to allow themselves to become so worn down, divided, and fragmented by such pressures to the extent that they forego their informed claims to bottom-line matters which are absolutely fundamental to positive educational experience.

Faculty should not stand in loco parentis except in the narrowest, legalistic sense. No student mistakes the realities of his or her relationship with parents with those of his or her relationship with teachers. The emotional factors are utterly and persuasively different. For anyone to assume that teachers stand in the place of parents is not only against nature, but it imposes altogether unfulfillable expectations on faculty and reduces by a significant measure their potential for guiding students' personal and intellectual growth. Accordingly, limits must be set regarding the familial role of the faculty in their interaction with students. Limits must also be set on what can be realistically expected of the educational structure and program. And faculties must set realistic limits on what they expect of themselves. In the end, school administrators, principals, department heads, committee members, and board members must set clear limits on how much time, energy, and concern faculty can reasonably deploy in the service of their students while at the same time preserving the necessary time, energy and concern for their own family and personal life. Without such clarification, the climate of the school can only deteriorate and with it the necessary ingredients not just for counseling, but for a basic and healthy educational setting.

As a practical matter, therefore, faculty and administration have an obligation to consider with the greatest seriousness the limits to be set in a school. Doing so is a difficult and complicated matter, for pressures always exist for elaborating academic programs, asking more of teachers, and promising more to students and families. Faculty committees are constantly reviewing and reformulating academic programs, but do they *ever* recommend cutting back curricula, making choices that limit what the school can *usefully* and most effectively offer, and abandoning those parts of the program which cannot be as effective as desired? These steps can free up enough faculty time and energy for them to pay appropriate attention to those aspects of the school program that can be effective. It simply is not necessary for *every* school to offer the broadest possible educational program. Overextending the faculty's commitments can create a school climate which is pressured—even a bit frantic—and which obliterates the essential ingredient of the educational process, namely, time for reflection. As knowledge, information, and techniques proliferate and as the demands and needs of society increase, somehow schools must reinforce basic educational and cognitive experience and, with it, the opportunity for personal growth. These fundamentals can be elaborated only to the extent that any given faculty has the personal, professional, and practical resources to do so while preserving the essential qualities and components of curricular relationships which make them truly educational. And so, faculties are—and should be—faced with hard choices and decisions. They need to evaluate all the possible ways of teaching and creating an educational system in a school and find an appropriate tradition, style, method, and curriculum which they can manage and make effective for their students in *their* circumstances and community. Such a program should be offered frankly and without shame or apology for its "incompleteness" or "limitations."

Currently, among many faculties there exists a sense of vulnerability. This feeling is due to many factors, among the most prominent of which are rapid and widespread change in educational schemes and systems, financial problems, rapid turnover (especially of headmasters, boards, and principals), and, most fundamentally, an increased ambivalence culturally about educational goals and processes. Good faculty relationships offset this sense of vulnerability, and they serve and enhance educational processes and purposes in a number of ways.

Faculty Relationships and Educational Purposes

Faculty need a healthy exchange of feelings as well as of ideas. This is not to suggest that the ordinary school be a rehabilitation center. Rather it is to argue for the validity of the affective side of learning that provides the growth-inducing thrust of healthy and vigorous intellectual pursuit. The latter is as important an aspect of educational experience for teachers as it is for students—in some cases, more so.

Second, cognitive process depends upon an emotional substrate, again for teachers as well as for students. A disrupted emotional process may disorder the thinking even of teachers, whereas a disciplined emotional process focuses the cognitive exchange between teachers and students and between teachers and teachers. It becomes, in a truly structural sense, the spine of effective education.

Third, it is important for teachers to personalize the educational process. They must know themselves as well as knowing their students, have some clear notions about their educational philosophy and values, and be willing to stand by them without imposing them on their students. And they need to take the time and make the effort to generate and support their own growth, both personally and professionally. If teachers are to be effective both in the classroom and outside it (where sometimes they have their greatest effect on students), they must attend to their own growth and the growth of their colleagues. Without that effort, education loses its zest, its flair, and its positive effect, becoming in the end a flat, uninspired, repetitive, and essentially useless and static routine.

In order to personalize the educational process, teachers must stress and exemplify reality—which is to say, reality as they perceive it—and be willing to discuss it, explore it and permit their perception of it to be examined, to change, to grow, and to mature. A teacher whose perception of reality is the same at the end of his or her career as it was at the beginning will not have provided a truly educational experience for the students. Part of that reality must be the inculcation of responsibility in students—assuming responsibility for their own behavior, decisions, choices, and intellectual process without manipulation. That can only happen if teachers freely and openly express and adhere to their value set, make clear what it is they approve of and disapprove of, express their judgments freely, and explore their own and their students' attitudes courageously. Above all, they must create an educational dialogue in which feelings have a legitimate role and sensitivity to feelings becomes a set of skills to be pursued as a lifetime task.

Chapter 7

COUNSELING UNDERACHIEVERS

Douglas H. Powell

An underachiever is a student whose academic performance is significantly below what might reasonably be expected. Just what constitutes a "significant" difference has sparked some debate among experts, but a rule of thumb is that an underachiever's level of performance is approximately 35 percentile points below that student's measured level of ability. For instance, comparison of a student's ability may show him to be in the top third of his class, but his three C's and a D place him in the bottom quarter. Or, a similar difference may be found between IQ and achievement test results.

We are not talking about youngsters with learning disabilities, attention deficit disorders, or significant constitutional factors which impair their ability to perform successfully in the classroom. The students under discussion here are typically of above average or better intelligence. In the pages ahead, we shall look at common manifestations of underachievement and then turn our attention to how teachers in the classroom can help these youngsters perform at a level more closely paralleling their ability.

Common Manifestations of Underachievement

Every classroom seems to have at least three types of underachievers: those who are low-risk takers, those who apparently are uncommitted, and those whose cognitive style seems at odds with the instructional mode of the teacher. These conditions are not causes of the academic problems; they are manifestations, rather like fever or swelling as evidence of an underlying physical problem. Let us look at how these youngsters behave in a classroom setting.

Low Risk Takers

These youngsters appear attentive and respectful, but are fearful of talking in class. Silent and unobtrusive, they never ask questions in class, never approach the teacher to find out what questions might be on an exam, and only rarely go over tests or papers they received back. As 16-year-old Seth put it, in response to an incomplete sentence test I gave him, "The *happiest time* is after I take a test . . . and before I get it back!" These students do not develop any perspective on how the teacher thinks, and therefore do not learn from failure. When called upon in class, they often look stricken. They may be unable to talk at all, or may blurt out the first thought that comes to mind as rapidly as possible.

Sometimes low risk takers can be identified by the way they talk about academic performance. Third person statements are common:

- The grades aren't coming.
- Things aren't working out.
- The studying isn't going as expected.
- The mark wasn't terrific.
- The term paper isn't getting written.

If one of these low-achieving youngsters uses the first person, it's often the first person *plural*, which has a way of diluting their involvement and commitment to the task. They will say, such things as, "We are not doing very well," or "We seem to be having a difficult time passing French," or "We have a hard time getting started writing a term paper." It is not clear whether they are using the editorial "we," the papal "we," the corporate "we," or the royal "we."

Then there are the low-achieving students who make contingency statements:

- As long as I keep studying, things will be OK.
- If I can write one page a day for the next two weeks, the paper will get done.
- Provided I stay motivated, the report card should turn out OK.

- There will be no problem if the reading for the course gets done.

Never does this student say, "*My* grades aren't what I want them to be," or "*I* am not fulfilling my expectations with my studying," or "*My* mark wasn't terrific." Neither do they tell us, "I intend to study for the exam," or "I plan to write a page a day." Rather, the motivation of these low risk takers seems to be fear of failure. In their hearts they are certain that if they try, they will fail and be humiliated. Thus, they avoid taking risks by not talking in class, by avoiding discussion of exams, and by ignoring their level of achievement; they seek to protect themselves from the frustration and humiliation that they imagine will be the cost of being committed. Approximately 50 percent of underachieving youngsters I see manifest this low-risk taking behavior.

The Uncommitted

These apparently indifferent underachievers make it clear to us by word and deed that they do not care, that they are relaxed and unmotivated. Obviously unenthusiastic about school, they can be found before exams watching television, playing cards, or shopping. They smilingly acknowledge, "I could do better if I tried," or "My grades don't reflect what I really know." Their behavior is especially challenging to teachers who value enthusiasm, excitement, caring, and commitment to the learning process.

The most frustrating aspect of these youngsters is that they seem to have a great deal of natural talent which they do not use on any consistent basis. The talent may be in athletics or singing. Yet, if a coach should tell Billy that he has the potential to be a first-string linebacker, the boy may respond by missing the next two practices. Should it be suggested to Hillary that she has an excellent alto voice and should try out for the choral society, she will be pleased to have her natural ability acknowledged but resist putting it to the test.

An interesting aspect of these apparently uncommitted youth is their fear that they might try their hardest and be discovered as merely somewhat better than average. A boy with a natural aptitude for science worries that if he commits himself to working hard in a chemistry course, he may make "only" a B + rather than an A if he tries his best—thus fracturing the illusion that he is extremely gifted but lazy.

When these youngsters try at all, they do it in secret. A girl in a boarding school was frustrated beyond words because her room-mate, Rebecca, seemed to make good grades in French without ever appearing to work at it. One night well after dark, prior to a mid-term exam, she woke up to hear a rustling in her closet. She opened the door to find Rebecca studying for the French exam with a flashlight.

Cognitive Style Problems

Some youngsters have difficulty in school because there is a "bad fit" between their learning style and that of many teachers. (By "learning style" we mean the way students habitually understand and organize knowledge.) Experts separate people into two groups with regard to which learning style—variously called left brain/right brain, percep-tual/conceptual, serialist/holist. In their unadulterated form, left brains are students who labor too hard to learn facts, master tech-niques, and understand logical sequences. They thrive on exam questions such as: "What was the date of the Magna Carta?" "What are the five steps in the scientific method?" Their knowledge, how-ever, is often without awareness of the frame of reference or points of observation that determine the origin or meaning of the data.

In contrast, pure right brains relate facts to a larger frame of ref-erence. They are interested in the origin of information and ideas and rely on intuitive judgment and reactions more than on hard data. They do very well on essay questions beginning with, "Compare and contrast . . . ," and attempt to display the inaccuracy of facts ("By whose calendar was the data of the Magna Carta signing recorded?") or show the naivete of the right answer ("Does any real scientist fol-low the five-step sequence of the scientific method?"). Capable stu-dents are both left- and right-brained and can adapt to the requirements of any course or teacher.

Unfortunately, some students overdevelop a particular learning style which causes them difficulty in class. For example, highly per-ceptual students have well-developed habits and are zealous, consci-entious, dutiful hard workers. When they have trouble, they assume that the number of hours they put in equals the grades that they will achieve. They prepare for classes with the same enthusiasm they show toward mowing the lawn. Their problem is that they are ex-tremely slow, guilt-ridden, obsessive, and compulsive; they have no understanding of what the teacher wants and have difficulty deciding on the correct answer because they see so many choices. (Multiple-choice tests are especially difficult for them.) They constantly lament that they studied 15 hours for an exam and got a C+, while their roommate who studied for only an hour and a half came out with an A−.

The roommate is likely to be a conceptual thinker. These are the youngsters who know the answers, as such, but not how to arrive at them. They are outstanding talkers, good reasoners, and excellent abstract thinkers, and they incisively cut to the heart of the matter. They often write beautifully—although the ink on their papers may still be wet when handed in. Their problem is that they have virtually no data. They lack habitual behavior, do things late or not at all, and often fail to live up to their promise. Sometimes these types of youngsters show remarkable intuitive ability. The best example of this case is Mr. Metzker. Mr. Metzker, a junior at Harvard concentrating in mathematics, enjoyed taking part in dramatic productions. One day he was waiting to take part in a rehearsal at Sanders Theater, but the rehearsal was canceled. As he was about to leave, he saw a friend entering the opposite hall to take a midterm exam in social science. Mr. Metzker extended appropriate condolences, then inquired what course his friend was being tested in. "Oh, Soc Si, something or other." "What's it all about?" asked Metzker. His friend replied, "It's about modern perspectives on man and society and all that."

"I've always wanted to take a course like that," said Metzker. "Any good reading?" His friend replied, "Yeah, there's this book. . . . " But his friend did not have time to finish.

"Take your seats," said a voice beside them. Their conversation by this time had taken them into the exam room, where both students automatically sat down. One proctor put blue books before them, and another gave them copies of a printed hour-long test.

Overwhelmed by a surge of curiosity and puckish glee, Mr. Metzker wrote "George Smith" on the blue book and addressed the first question.

Several days later, Mr. Metzker's friend picked up his own blue book and found himself in the company of most of his class receiving a C+. Quietly, he picked up "George Smith's" blue book.

When they looked at it, they found that Mr. Metzker had gotten a D on those sections with objective or spot questions—largely due to his sophistication in the theory of probability. What was astonishing, however, was that on the last half of the exam he received an A− for the essay. The teacher's comments read, "Excellent work. You could have pinned down the observations a bit more, but. . . . " The news could not be contained. The next day's *Crimson* revealed the scandal. In an interview with that student newspaper, Metzker said that there was really nothing to it. The essay question asked the student to discuss one of two books: Margaret Meade's *And Keep Your Powder Dry* or, Geoffrey Gorer's *The American People*. Two critical comments were offered on each book, one favorable and one unfavorable. Though having read neither of them, Metzker said that he chose the second because "the title gave me some notion as to what the book might be about."

He took his first cue from the name Geoffrey and committed himself to the premise that Gorer was born into an Anglo-Saxon culture—maybe English, certainly English-speaking. Having heard that Margaret Meade was a social anthropologist, he inferred that Gorer was in the same field. Then he began the essay by centering his inquiry upon what might be probable in an anthropologist's observation of a culture close to his own. Drawing partly upon memories of table talk in his dormitory and partly from creative logic, he rang changes on the relationship of the observer to the observed, assessing the degree of objectivity on the part of an observer trained as an anthropologist.

At the end, he concluded that the book did contribute a range of "objective" and even "fresh" insights into the nature of our culture. "At the same time," he warned, "these observations must be understood within the context of their generation by a person only partly freed from his embeddedness in the culture he is observing and limited in his capacity to transcend these particular tendencies and biases which he has himself developed as a personality in his interaction with his culture since his birth. In this sense, the book portrays as much the character of Geoffrey Gorer as it analyzes that of the American people."[1]

Helping Students with Learning Problems

No catalog of proven cures or pharmacopoeia of remedies exists to help students with learning problems. What we have is accumulated

---

[1] William G. Perry, Jr., "Examsmenship and the Liberal Arts: A Study in Educational Epistemology," in L. Bramson (ed.), *Examining Harvard College: A Collection of Essays by Members of the Harvard Faculty* (Cambridge, Mass.: Harvard University Faculty of Arts and Sciences, 1963).

experience from generations of teachers and clinicians who have worked successfully with troubled youngsters. Let us discuss some general principles and specific types of interventions that are useful with young people such as these.

General Principles

The first principle for helping a student with a learning problem is to stay in contact. It is impossible to help someone without your physical presence. Assisting someone to overcome a learning problem requires a relationship. No matter what we do, a bond between teacher and student must exist.

The second principle is to involve the student. Helping a boy or girl overcome a learning problem is not something we do *to* them; it is something we do *with* them. Often, involving students in helping them recognize their problems encourages them to use their own creative energies to see what they can do to overcome the difficulty. It also creates an important and necessary sense of sharing and responsibility.

The third principle is to look at the data involving reports, grades, teachers' comments, and test scores as far back as records exist. Many times a youngster's difficulty in school can be traced to a specific trauma—for example, Billy started having trouble in mathematics as a fourth-grader when his teacher was killed in a car accident. Some students develop negative identities which start things going down hill. Is a sixth-grade girl really not able to do mathematics, or have there been marital problems, a move to a new city which has triggered a depression, or a sudden change in family pressure which has resulted in poor grades? Sometimes the data do not particularly inform us of the reasons for an academic problem, but many times they do.

The fourth principle is to do one thing at a time. With a youngster who has problems across the board, it does very little good to attack everything at once. It is best to pick a target symptom and work toward relieving that. If a youngster is having trouble with math computation, focus on that particular problem, even though so doing means ignoring for the moment difficulties with handwriting, spelling, and foreign language. The student might, likewise, be encouraged to turn papers in on time, to talk in class, or to force himself to study as much as two hours per night.

The fifth principle is to schedule short periods of evaluation. It is not unusual for students to make a sudden spurt of improvement after receiving help but then quickly slide back to their old ways. Scheduling regular evaluations—at the end of every week or month—enables the teacher to keep track of whether the interventions are being useful and also gives the youngster an opportunity to monitor his or her own progress.

The sixth principle is to not be afraid to make changes. Often, the solving of a youngster's difficulty in math, for example, should be approached as one would focus a camera. Some fine tuning often needs to be employed to help a youngster with test anxiety. Sometimes a major change is needed. If a student is unable to study two hours a night, an alternative is to break up that period into 20-minute units, with breaks between so that the two hours of study is eventually accomplished during the day.

The seventh principle is to keep trying different approaches. It is not crucial that an intervention match specifically the diagnosis of the problem. Studies of interventions that were not quite perfect show that they are often successful. This is reminiscent of the famous Hawthorne effect, which demonstrates that doing anything—sometimes even the wrong thing—can have beneficial results. We never know what it is we might say or do that might be helpful. I recall a sixth-grade teacher of mine who was encouraging me to enter a writing contest. She said, "Doug, I know that I will read something by you some day." I do not remember whether I entered the contest, and I surely did not win, but those words have an effect on me to this day.

Finally, should improvement occur, one should not be too enthusiastic. Comments should be lukewarm, such as, "You did reasonably well." Inquire as to the student's reactions, "How do you feel about this progress?" Many youngsters who begin to make some improvement feel it imperative to continue, and they worry that they cannot keep it up. Expect regression: No matter how effective an initial intervention, it is human nature to fall back. Students should be alerted to this possibility and not punished when it occurs.

Specific Interventions

Low Risk Takers

With low risk takers, the goal is to change behavior. This begins with an assessment of why they are reluctant to take risks in the classroom.

Reasons include fears of being wrong or thought stupid, overachieving and being ridiculed by an esteemed but underachieving group of peers, and inability to live up to what they imagine to be the demands of their parents.

A program for risk taking should be established. One example is to encourage the student to talk in class. The adviser could tell the student that he or she is expected to speak in each of his or her classes. Those who are especially reluctant can be asked to record opportunities they see to talk in class by making a small "O" on the left-hand margin of their class notes. When they take an opportunity to speak, they can put a slash through the "O." This approach is often fruitful, for simply observing our behavior changes it. If, for example, one who has the habit of biting fingernails records the number of instances of fingernail-biting in the course of the day, the frequency of the habit may well diminish.

Questioning should be encouraged. Many youngsters are fearful of asking a question in class for fear of revealing themselves to be unsophisticated. They also have the fantasy that if they ask a question, the teacher will punish them for not knowing the material. It is useful to solicit questions from low risk takers both during the class and afterward.

Finally, it is well to encourage anticipation of what might be on the examination. Students should be encouraged to talk to other students or to study with them in groups prior to an examination. The teacher should review mistakes made on early examinations with these students and explain how their perception of the desired answer fell short. Such students should be urged to think about what the teacher may see as the most valuable material on a potential examination. And, finally, if they are available, prior examinations should be reviewed by the student.

Students with Immature Work Habits

A sign once posted in the weight room at Clemson University said something to the effect that "the difference between good and great is just a little extra effort." That message struck me as being wrong, because the difference between good and great actually seems to require an enormous amount of extra effort—especially in the classroom. A good example is the enormous amount of effort required to help a youngster who lacks good work habits. Such a student must learn to do a lot of little things differently, and this learning process requires a great deal of effort on the teacher's part as well.

The first step in helping somebody with this problem is to do everything possible to reinforce habituated behavior. The student should schedule his or her time for the week, including rest periods, visiting with friends, and studying. Each day should have a checklist which should be marked at the end of every 24 hours.

The student's personal life/habits should be disciplined. This involves setting up a daily order of getting out of bed, going to the bathroom, washing one's hands, brushing one's teeth, taking a shower, et cetera. It also involves organization of one's room, desk drawers, and closet. Most students have no sense of how a desk should be ordered, to say nothing of their closets.

The teacher should help them find formulas for writing papers and breaking down large projects into doable units. Often this means starting with the face sheet of a paper, helping them learn where to put the title, their name, and the date, as well as the name of the teacher and the course. There are a number of useful books which describe—although somewhat woodenly—systems for writing papers.

Excess stimulation such as loud music, general noise, or phone calls should be reduced, for youngsters who lack habituated behavior seem to be overresponsive to any outside stimulus.

Frequent short contacts should be arranged for monitoring behavior. For many students this can be 3 to 5 minutes, 5 days a week. This is the time to go over their checklists and encourage them to anticipate their organizational requirements for the day/week. A reward system can be negotiated with the individual, but it must be done on at least a weekly basis.

Despite all these efforts, however, it is difficult for youngsters who lack habituated behavior patterns to develop them. It is not a matter of desire and willpower alone, but a matter of lengthy practice. Moreover, many of these students come to the school with immature work habits.

The Apparently Uncommitted

The objective in dealing with uncommitted students is to break into their numbness. This process, which has been called "anxiety eliciting therapy," gets them to worry more and use this tension to stimulate themselves to study.

Many teachers use this technique—for example, the French teacher who screams at her students, "How dare you come into my class unprepared. Don't you know how important it is for me that you learn this material?" Professor Rassia at Dartmouth uses another technique, which involves the students emotionally in mastering a foreign language.

The more the teacher can do to encourage such worrying, the better off these students will be. A manageable level of anticipatory anxiety will trigger studying and preparation. I once worked with a student who always seemed in very good spirits and relaxed before he went into the examination. It took me several months to realize that he was not worrying enough. As soon as we got him to worry properly, his anxiety level motivated him not only to study more effectively but to keep his edge while he was taking the exam.

In this connection, it is very important that when students study, they are not just covering the ground. They should master the concepts and learn the material, not just turn the pages.

It is also important in dealing with these students to remember that no one lacks motivation in all areas. Finding something positive that they are doing outside classroom—a service activity, a sport, or working—opens the way to reinforcing their motivation.

Helping Students with Cognitive Style Problems

Students having a perceptual style problem should be shifted from a quantity to a quality orientation. Less will be more. They need to focus on getting the idea of the material in order to master it, rather than simply putting in long hours covering the ground. One thing they should realize is that it is not the number of hours put into studying for an exam that counts, but how these hours are used.

In this regard, obsessive note taking should be discouraged. Often, information goes straight from the ears to the hand and becomes written notes, without passing through the brain. One helpful approach is to have them listen for 5 minutes to get the sense of a lecture before taking any notes. Highlighting should also be discouraged. Many students actually highlight the entire book.

Overly high-level expectations tend to be another problem of perceptual problem students. They need often to scale down their expectations in order to do a simple, workmanlike job.

Students with conceptual problems need to be taught behavior organizational tricks, as well as rigor. The teacher should not be too understanding. These students must learn what to do when their intuition fails. The teacher can help them deal with breaking a problem into manageable units and encourage them to write regularly.

While we are struggling to help underachievers, it is sometimes helpful to remember three points. The first is that youngsters having trouble in school are not doing it on purpose; they would rather be making honors grades. The second point is that most of the successful people in North America were not academic stars. This is because life makes very different demands on us than school, rewarding human qualities that are not so easily graded on a report card. Finally, it is important not to let the failure of students you are trying to help fracture the bond of caring between you. Youngsters may not be ready to be helped when you make your effort. School gives young people lots of second chances. A year later, or a decade later, the memory of your advice, and, more importantly, the memory of your advice in a caring relationship, may make an enormous difference in someone's life.

Chapter 8

TALKING WITH PARENTS

Graham B. Blaine, Stanley H. King, and Preston K. Munter

"We simply cannot be expected to make anything of Jason, given the kind of family he has."
"That school is simply not doing their job with Jason."

Such passing of the buck is all too familiar in difficult school situations. The causes and remedies are intimately connected. As is the case with so many of the difficulties students have in school, the culprit is frequently not the student but, rather, inaccurate, or insufficient information. Schools all too often adopt an unrealistically optimistic stance toward troubled students, taking the slightest sign of improvement as an indication that there is no longer need to worry. They thus miss an opportunity to inform parents early enough for them to assist in remedying whatever may be causing difficulty for the student. Just as often, parents fail to keep in touch with what is going on at school and become aware that there is trouble only when grades are sent to them. Some parents make matters worse by ignoring warnings relayed to them by deans and advisers, particularly when the student dismisses them as not serious.

But there are other reasons why this gridlock develops between parents and schools. Perhaps Jason persuaded his teachers that his parents are unusually punitive and that he will be cruelly treated if they are brought in. Or perhaps the school authorities have been intimidated by the family, on the one hand lending some credibility to the student's fears, and on the other making school administrators and teacher, alike, reluctant to risk bringing down the fury of parents on their heads. Less commonly, a problem may arise when there is a divorce and notices are sent to parents in separate parts of the country or the world. A "Let George do it" attitude may result, where each partly feels that the other either is dealing or should be dealing with the problem; in the end, neither responds.

Actually, most parent-related problems center on two mistaken premises: first, that parents do not have much effect on children's behavior during adolescence; and second, that parents are incapable of changing their attitudes. There has always been controversy about the relative impact of nature and nurture on growth and development. Views vary along a continuum from proponents of "As the twig is bent, so the tree is inclined," to those who believe in the life-crippling effect of a traumatic event. Of course, genes play a part in personality development, as do modeling by parents and the various losses, disappointments, and disillusionments encountered throughout life. How much each factor influences the development of an individual is truly indeterminable and, for our purposes, may be quite unimportant. What does matter is that changes in parental attitudes can promote a positive turnaround in the behavior of a child.

Impact of the Student's Struggle for Autonomy

In many cases, the interactions between parents and son or daughter reflect the struggle for autonomy and independence that is part of adolescent growth. That struggle can result in the two sides becoming deadlocked—not willing to modify their positions and each critical of the other. If parents can take the lead—especially with the help of a concerned teacher—in trying to understand better what is going on and in opening a constructive dialogue with their offspring, there can be positive results in the student's attitude and behavior. Improvement in the student can result from an increase in self-esteem and a feeling that important people care and that the student's feelings and ideas are being acknowledged and respected. Accomplishing this improvement may not be easy, either because of the intensity of anger on the part of the student or because of fear on the part of the parents that yielding will lead to loss of control. It is easy for whoever is the object of anger to feel that acceding to the student's wishes will only increase the anger or that the student will only be provoked to increase his or her negative attitudes and behavior. The task of the teacher in this situation is a delicate one: to acknowledge to the parents that they, too, are angry or perhaps afraid, but also that they want the best for their son or daughter and that taking some risks may induce positive change. An acknowledgment of anger is also in order with the student, but the teacher can help the student see a potential payoff in entering into a dialogue, especially one in which it can be made clear that, despite the negative feelings, there is also reality in the degree of caring. This happens often enough so that, when trouble arises for a given student, a concerted effort is warranted on the part of teachers and administrators to achieve the cooperation of his or her parents.

When both parents do respond to a request for a conference, it is important to anticipate that parents commonly expect teachers to blame them for whatever problem the child may have. From the outset, it is often helpful to point out that assessing blame avails nothing and that doing so is not the purpose of the parent-teacher conference. The objective, rather, is to bring out the best in the student and to work out joint plans to accomplish this end. After the here-and-now situation is clearly delineated and discussion has, hopefully, clarified misunderstandings about the nature of the student's problem, the parents should be asked for suggestions as to what measures might be taken to bring about improvement. These suggestions should give the teacher a clearer understanding of the nature of the relationship between the parents and their child, which very often turns out to be quite different from the picture the student has presented.

In dealing specifically with the areas where help can be effectively given, it sometimes turns out that we are faced with choices representing exact opposites. Following are some suggestions which can be made to parents who are working with teachers to help a student who is struggling with academic or disciplinary problems.

Adjusting Expectations

Helping parents talk through their expectations for the student will enable them to accept a more realistic level of possible achievements—that is, a level compatible with the student's abilities. Pushing for A's from a student who has a perfectly respectable average IQ leads only to frustration and discouragement. If persistent, such pressures can lead to serious depression and a total shutdown of cognitive process. On the other hand, parental lack of interest in academic achievement can cause a student to give up. Sometimes parents need to be more accepting of the level at which their child functions effectively, while at other times they need to exhibit more genuine interest in the attainments of their offspring.

Parental Participation

Another way for teachers and parents to work collaboratively on the problems students have at school is to find ways of parental participation in school activities. Sometimes students feel that the school world in which they live and with which they interact is totally separate from the world in which their parents live and work. This leads to a sense of isolation, of having to accomplish obligatory or elective tasks without having either interest or appreciation from those at home. To counter this sense of disconnection, a sensitive teacher may work with both student and parents on the task of reconnection. In this task the feelings of disappointment and frustration by the student will need to be addressed and conveyed in some manner to the parents. The teacher may be able to act as the student's advocate in this process, but will need to be careful to present the situation in an objective, not a critical, manner. The mode should be one of collaboration to solve a problem, rather than an adversarial approach. If student, teacher, and parents can become engaged in a dialogue that is focused on understanding and change, parental behavior in terms of participation may change for the better. The dialogue may need to confront some realities, particularly of time and distance in a boarding school situation, or the demands of a father's work that keep him away from home excessively. But there may be other factors such as the potentially negative impact on family cohesion in dual-career households. Differences in interests between parents and student, perhaps reflecting conflicting value orientations at the moment, may also be impediments to parental participation.

Working through such differences will not be accomplished quickly or easily, especially if much of it has to be done on the telephone. But once again, the central task is having a dialogue that considers feelings as well as time and that tries to keep in central focus the ongoing development and well-being of the student. One or both of the parents may find that telephone conversations about school work or a show of interest in what the student is doing in class or laboratory can be helpful. In a day school, those conversations may take place over the dinner table or on the weekends. Whether the participation is of this kind or is attending student functions, the net result can be the student's feeling that what she or he is doing is of some significance to important people in his or her life—that there is a reconnection.

Excessive Parental Intervention

There are, of course, instances where excessive parental interest can inhibit productive performance by leading to the student's sense of being suffocated or pressured. In such cases, teachers need to help parents withdraw and allow the school to handle whatever student problems may be coming to the surface. It is not at all uncommon or surprising that the words of the consulting therapist, "Leave it up to the school," often bring relief of tension on both sides. This is particularly true in situations where the school has to impose structure and rules and, thus, necessary discipline, for example, unfinished homework assignments, tardiness, and missed appointments. In these situations strong parental feelings may be displaced onto the school. Parents may want the school to take a tough stand—even to be punitive—or they may be critical of the teacher or administration if the discipline is not as severe as the parent thinks necessary. In most cases the school can be grateful for solid support of this kind from parents, but there are times when the student will feel it as an intrusion, another type of suffocation, or inappropriate pressure. The issue of rules and discipline is not at stake here; rather it is how the discipline is imposed on a particular student.

Sometimes there are difficulties in the student-parent interactions to the point where the student feels burdened by parental participation. The task of the teacher or administrator is once again to open a dialogue, to respond to the feelings on both sides, and to center the dialogue on what is going on with the student and how the student's growth and behavior can be enhanced. Teachers and administrators may have some reluctance to foster such dialogue, fearing the intransigence of parents and the danger of eliciting an angry response from them. Two factors are relevant to overcoming this fear. First, the intransigence and potential anger can often be prevented or muted by acknowledging the feelings on both sides, allowing their expression, and discussing them until they have softened and both student and parents can see beyond them. Second, teachers often underestimate the flexibility of parents, just as parents underestimate the flexibility of teachers and both may underestimate the student. If the teacher opens the dialogue with the expectation of reasonableness—of the possibility for greater understanding of the situation once feelings have been explored—the opportunity for change and progress is substantial.

Limit Setting

Perhaps the most important area for school-parent cooperation is setting limits on the behavior of students. Often there is considerable disparity in the value system of a school and that of the family in which a student may have spent the earlier years of his or her life. Limit setting under these circumstances may be annoying and frustrating to the student, and it may not receive support on the part of parents that the school desires. In dealing with parents about limit setting, the teacher or administrator will find it helpful to remember the value of limit setting both for the growth and development of the adolescent and for the sense of community in the school. Structure and rules are one way of expressing the underlying values which give an organization or community its sense of purpose and being. When the purpose is clear and strong, the members of the community benefit, taking some of that strength into themselves. Self-esteem and a sense of identity in an adolescent can be enhanced by participating in a community with such purpose. Enforcement of rules, or limit setting, is a way of restating the purpose of the community and of the relationship of the individual to that community. At the same time, the setting of limits can be useful to the adolescent in dealing with powerful feelings and impulses when there may be conflict in the adolescent about ways in which these impulses should be expressed. As indicated in Chapter 3, some adolescents may feel turmoil in trying to find a way through this conflict. Clear limits, and their enforcement, can reduce such turmoil, although teachers and administrators should be prepared for an adversarial response by the student, at least initially. The value of limit setting in counseling is noted in Chapter 2 and Chapter 6. It should, and can be, a growth-enhancing experience for any given student.

Remembering this may help the teacher to be consistent and to stay focused on the central issue of the growth of the student in dealing with parents about limit setting. The goal is to seek close collaboration between parents and the school, even when there is disparity in values and lifestyle. Acknowledgment of disparity without being critical or censurious is the first step in building collaboration. In so doing, teachers must not underestimate the flexibility or goodwill of parents, especially when their wishes for the success of their offspring can be mobilized. A constructive dialogue of benefit to the student is usually possible.

Attempting to enforce compliance to a rule by temporary suspension, for instance, is strikingly ineffective if the student involved returns home to an environment where he is allowed to indulge that behavior at will. For example, a young man was sent home for breaking the rule against chewing tobacco. His parents thought the punishment inappropriate, as did their son, and they did nothing to discourage his chewing. When it came time for his return to school, the young man refused to sign the agreement to refrain from chewing, despite the fact that his return was contingent upon his doing so. At that point his parents and the school began serious communication, in the course of which his mother learned of the dangerous consequences of chronic oral tobacco use. At the school's suggestion, she made an appointment for her son with his physician and also withdrew a number of privileges such as use of the car and his personal television set. Soon the young man came to understand the risks he was running and, with some difficulty, broke himself of the addiction. In this instance, the agreement of the school and the parents about the nature of the problem and their mutual agreement to set firm limits made a satisfactory and effective resolution possible.

Completing Assignments

In dealing with students who simply refuse to do homework or complete written assignments or those who make promises to do so but then complain that they are distracted, cannot concentrate, or are too busy with more important obligations, schools and parents often find themselves working at cross-purposes. It is important in such instances to clearly define areas of responsibility. In the majority of cases, assigning the full burden to the school seems to work best. Then the normal rebellion against family is bypassed and only the transferred resistance to authority serves as a barrier to compliance. The latter is usually less in degree than the former.

"Transferred resistance" is a term describing the shift in the student's struggle for autonomy and independence from the parents to the school, wherein teachers and administrators are seen—quite unconsciously—by the student as parental figures. The struggle can be localized and thus often reduced in intensity if parents and school both understand what is going on and decide together that the school should handle it. When communication between parent and school is good, they do not work at cross-purposes. If they can agree on a course of action, then the school can concentrate on setting limits, responding to the student's feelings, and helping the student work through these feelings.

A case in point is that of Mark, the eldest son of a successful lawyer. Mark did reasonably well in elementary school, but when he started at his father's school, a private secondary high school, he began to falter. His father became more and more angered by his son's poor performance, particularly his lack of effort. In an attempt to help, the father began to supervise his son's homework and to tutor him in math. This led to violent arguments between them, and there was no improvement in Mark's grades. It also led Mark to lie about assignments and the grades he attained on quizzes. Finally, the school asked Mark to leave because of his low achievement. He was sent to another independent boarding school where he was much happier and seemed to be doing well. However, at first marking period he turned up with failing grades in four out of five courses. His teachers complained that he did not hand in papers, yawned openly in class, and indeed fell asleep in class—all the time professing to be trying hard to do well and to want to succeed. Toward the end of his first year, he was required to leave because of blatant defiance of the rules against drinking. When Mark returned home he was placed in a local tutoring or "cram" school where the policy regarding homework assignments was absolutely rigid: You stayed at school until the work was done, even if that meant remaining until midnight. No excuses for missing school except dire illness could prevent a student from spending a Saturday in the classroom. Mark's grades at this school astounded the family (4 A's and a B) and enabled him to gain admission to an appropriate college.

This vignette illustrates the value of adapting a homework program to the special needs of individual parent-child situations. Here, relegating total responsibility to the school was the right answer. In other instances, shared responsibility or a cooperative effort of some kind may be the solution to the same or a similar problem.

Anti-Intellectualism

Some parents have limited respect for or interest in scholarship or intellectual achievement. This is more likely to occur in upwardly mobile families where the parents may have had a very limited education themselves and have achieved economic success through hard work and an intuitive ability often referred to as "street smarts." Sometimes it occurs in families with established wealth where the emphasis is on social activities rather than achievement and performance. On an unconscious level these parents may have some contempt for teachers and scholarship, which they view as less relevant to the "real" world. Often contempt is mixed with envy of intellectual power—and perhaps some fear of it. These unconscious feelings and conflicts may be reflected in conscious thought and behavior that downplays academic success by their children and in a defensiveness about the emphasis that the school places on academic achievement. Outward behavior may be subtle in nature, reflected in off-hand remarks to the student that demean academic work or in planning social activities that take the student away from academic pursuits. The defensiveness evident in such behavior and attitudes of parents can have negative effects on the achievement of their offspring, especially if that student is bright, and it certainly can produce frustration and anger on the part of teachers. Anti-intellectualism is obviously counter to the central purpose of a school. Because the negative feelings about scholarship on the part of parents are usually unconscious, the parents often provide mixed messages to the student. By sending him or her to the school, they appear to value intellectual endeavor; by subtly or directly demeaning academic work, they devalue academics.

The negative effects of anti-intellectualism on the student may take several forms. In some students there may be an increase in conflict with the parents, leading to anger and rebellion. Because the parents do not realize that they are giving mixed messages, they may be especially puzzled by their offspring's anger. Some students react with erratic academic performance—that is, high one term and low the next, or good marks in some courses and poor marks in others. In other cases, academic performance may be substantially less than teachers think possible on the basis of test scores and class interactions. Either erratic or low performance can reflect the confusion the student feels about what is expected of him or her by the parents.

The task of the teacher or administrator dealing with such students is to explore the possibility that the parents may be conveying mixed messages, or clear negative ones. School and parents should work together to understand the situation and discuss how parents might change their behavior. If the feelings of the parents are largely unconscious, it will take several conferences for an adequate exploration. The key to success lies in conveying the idea of collaboration for the good of the student. In so doing, the teacher or administrator will need to monitor his or her own feelings of anger that the educational purpose of the school is being undermined. There are occasions in dealing with parents when silence has virtue.

Another aspect of attitude toward academic achievement is some students' fear of surpassing their parents. This unconscious fear can be based on a number of factors. The student may fear that parental love will be withdrawn if he or she exceeds the parents' attainments, or may feel that one or both parents are not strong enough to deal with their offspring's success. Such fears can interfere with the student's academic achievement.

A variation on this theme can occur when the student has a sibling who is either much brighter or much less accomplished intellectually. If the sibling is brighter, the student may eschew academic striving, perhaps fearful that any effort in that direction will only emphasize the differences between them. Under these circumstances it is not uncommon for a student to work well below his or her capacity or even to appear contemptuous of intellectual pursuits. If the sibling is less intelligent, the student may feel pressure—usually in subtle ways—from the parents to limit academic striving in order to prevent feelings of inferiority on the part of the less-gifted sibling.

Before working with parents on these issues, the teacher should spend some time with the student in question to explore the feelings of fear. The student will not be able to change in any significant degree until these feelings have been worked through and teacher, student, and parents can confront the problems together. If the student can talk about his or her fears with the parents, they in turn may be able to express their concerns. A danger to which the teacher should be alert is an attempt by the parents to reassure the student before the problem has been fully explored. Such premature reassurance often has a hollow ring and does not help the student; in fact, it only obscures the problem. Patient dialogue, in which the teacher helps both student and parents to look at the problem from different angles, brings out feelings on both sides, and keeps the focus on the central problem—all without being judgmental—can often be of substantial help to both student and parents.

Divorce

Teachers can play a vitally important role as mediator when divorce occurs in a student's family. Sometimes a faculty member senses that a divorce is imminent either in the course of parent contact or as evidenced by a student's words or behavior. It is best to take such indicators seriously, for young people are always deeply affected by the separation or divorce of parents. Loss of the family is experienced as a real loss; indeed, it may be as upsetting as a death. Elsewhere in this book the manner in which a death in the family can best be dealt with is well covered; similar measures should be taken in the case of students whose parents divorce. In addition, attention must be paid to the ensuing alteration in the family constellation—for example, one should not look to one of the separated parents as the only parent. This situation may lead to painful confrontations for the student, who may have to be the bearer of information which one parent may have either unintentionally or spitefully kept from the other.

In dealing with parents where divorce is involved, the teacher must keep in mind the principle described in Chapters 1 and 2, on the counseling process: Approach the counseling interaction without being judgmental. Often the teacher will find this difficult, because the temptation to take sides or hold opinions about parental behavior is very strong. If the teacher considers the behavior of one of the parents immoral or destructive to the student, it will be tempting to introduce this in the interaction with that parent. Also, if the teacher talks with each parent separately it will be tempting to share the feeling of judgment with the aggrieved party. The student is not well served by this. In working with the parents, either separately or together, the teacher will need to keep them focused on the idea that the well-being of the student is the central issue. Observable effects of parental tension and anger on the student can be brought out, with as much objectivity and lack of negative judgment as possible. Attention should be given to the actions necessary to alter the effect on the student. By keeping the focus on the student, the teacher can avoid becoming the object of parental anger and manipulation.

There is, of course, the danger that teachers will be caught in the crossfire between parents as they work out their hostilities toward each other. Some seek to use the teacher as a pawn or ally, much as they try to do with the student. When this happens, the parents need to be confronted with their behavior, using a limit-setting approach. The teacher should comment about what she or he thinks is going on, cite the evidence as clearly and objectively as possible, and note the destructive results of the behavior on the student. The teacher will also need to make it clear that she or he cannot be helpful to the student when caught in the crossfire. As in any kind of counseling situation, the confrontation should be done with firmness, coupled with concern.

In dealing with divorce situations, the interaction with parents often can be enhanced by the involvement of more than one person from the school. Two heads may be better than one in helping to keep calm; one person may think of something that has escaped the other; and a stronger front can be maintained for keeping the focus on the student. A dual approach also helps to ease the strain on individual teachers. The team should involve the teacher who knows the student best and include also someone from the administration. These people may want to discuss the matter with the school's psychological consultant before talking with the parents, and in some cases, they may want to bring the consultant into the sessions directly.

Conclusion

In closing, it is important to give one caveat and one suggestion. Students are often quite adept at portraying their parents in a light that is to the student's best advantage but not entirely accurate or fair. Teachers and therapists alike have been surprised when confronted face-to-face with compassionate and sensitive parents who had been described in detail over the years as cruel and unyielding. To excuse behavior on the basis of clearly established cruel and abusive treatment at home is one thing; to modify a school's disciplinary processes and procedures by accepting a distorted picture of conditions at home is another.

This situation provides an opportunity for a counseling interaction with both parents and the student. The task is to understand why the student is portraying the parental behavior in such a negative manner. The teacher can explore possible reasons with the parents and discuss developmental issues and what subsurface stresses that may be causing problems for the student. With the student, the teacher can explore feelings and behavior with a stance of puzzlement, wondering with the student what is at the root of it all. Eventually, a dialogue among all the parties concerned may help to change behavior, but that is likely only after exploratory work has been done with both parents and students.

As a final suggestion, schools should seriously consider providing an orientation period for parents and students at the start of each year. It is likely to be very helpful to schedule a time to meet with parents and students together in order to know them as a family and to develop a sense of the family style and the nature of the family interactions. Most important, this provides an opportunity for parents and teachers to understand expectations on both sides and to develop collaboratively a realistic picture of what lies ahead.

Chapter 9

TECHNICAL ISSUES IN COUNSELING

Jane H. Leavy

Recently, a young woman talked with me about her difficulty in feeling good about herself. She was distressed that the personal relationships in her life, while very improved over the past few years, were still troubled and unfulfilling. It was mid-May. Her graduate school courses were over for the semester, and she was waiting for the summer semester to begin. She agreed with the observation that things always seemed more difficult when school was not in session, adding, "There were always some teachers who noticed when I did well."

This woman, who grew up in a very troubled and unhappy family, always experienced school as a place where there was a structure in which she could find a way to "do well," as she put it, where she could be appreciated, where she could grow, and where there was real refuge from the destructive and undercutting effects of her family's relationship with her. There was nothing special about her school experience as a child. She went to a strict Catholic elementary school and a large urban high school, where she had very few friends, but she did good work and got good grades, and some teachers noticed. That was what school really was all about. Some of her teachers took an interest in her, noticed that she had some real talents, and found a way, despite her shy, somewhat depressed demeanor, to let her know that they valued her.

143

This person is by no means unique. Many adults describe an experience of this kind. School, unlike home, was a place where they felt whole, where they felt appreciated, where they felt they were being judged fairly. In the school environment, teachers—not the institution—are the attraction for such people. Teachers are the ones who bring people out, teach them to value themselves, and notice when they do well. Adults tell about the power these relationships have had in their lives and how these relationships made the difference between feeling, on the one hand, that there was nobody there and, on the other hand, that there was somebody interested, committed, and exerting a uniquely positive influence on self-esteem. It is the job of the therapist to take up where these teachers leave off.

The relationship between students and teachers is the subject of this chapter. We shall discuss what goes on in the relationship as it grows and develops, what sustains it, and what limits it, as well as review some concepts to think about and standards to consider. The parameters of our discussion will include both the formal, long-term counseling relationships with a student or two and the more casual relationships with students that assume a personal meaning for the student and teacher. For the sake of brevity, we will call both "counseling relationships," understanding that many of them are likely to be carried out in the intermittent, informal ways that such things happen in schools. We will address certain technical issues that arise when teachers work closely with a student, and when the teacher and the student become aware that the relationship is valued by both. What rules apply here? How does the teacher gauge whether such a relationship is good for the student? How does the student experience the relationship? Where have things gone wrong, if they have? What about the teacher's feelings for the student? And when is it time to let go?

Some of what follows will be a continuation of the discussion in Chapter 1. In this chapter we shall focus on four principles essential to the work of counseling which counselors in training need to track closely. These principles (which have technical names in the lexicon of mental health) are neutrality, transference, confidentiality, and termination. We shall define and clarify those terms, and use other terminology as well in a discussion of openness, the interpersonal field, respecting of boundaries, and helping students grow and go away.

The Principle of Neutrality

When someone comes into my office, I have usually not met him or her before. I have been given some information by whomever has made the referral, but I begin with no first-hand knowledge of the person. I form an impression very quickly, however, categorizing, judging, and labelling—often on the basis of little information and always with the bias that I personally bring.

The point is that under these circumstances, one has to watch out. People who work with students have access to a great deal of information that can create an impression even before the student opens his or her mouth. The teacher may have seen the student in class, or colleagues may have made comments on the student's ability or behavior. There is a file on the student's life since kindergarten. The student may have been preceded by a sibling or two, or the teacher may know the parents. The student may be a star in the school, or a loser. But, one way or another, the teacher often knows the student as a *somebody* even before the initial meeting.

Our sense of who a person is, what he or she needs from us, and what that person should do is often formed by the ways an individual fits into our preformed notions about people in general. No one is, by nature, neutral about other people. Everyone has had too much experience—good and bad—in personal relationships and in interpersonal dealings to perceive a newly met person neutrally. Teachers, like everyone else, bring to their encounters with students all of their previous relationships, all of their prejudices, all of their limitations, and sometimes their fantasies or hopes.

When the distortions that we bring to forming an impression of a person lead us to prejudge, to exclude some things from our awareness, or to attend to our own overriding agendas for a person's life, counseling cannot take place. Such distortions create an urgency in the situation, in that we constantly feel compelled to make that person be who we think he or she is. So we give a lot of advice and try to take care of their troubles for them, and sometimes, when we cannot get them to do it our way, we give up on them.

The concept of neutrality in counseling is a challenge to these natural tendencies in all of us. It challenges us to acknowledge our own preconceptions openly, and then set them aside. It requires that we make an effort to minimize the distortions in what we see by making the necessary corrections in our personal view of things. "Neutrality" is not a condition of having no feelings for people, or not having hope that they do well, or not caring deeply. It is, rather, a state of self-knowledge and awareness of the difference between really understanding someone and merely perceiving a version of the person that we have created in our own imagination.

The principle of neutrality implies certain standards or rules in the practice of counseling which deserve attention. The four which follow are particularly relevant to the counseling situation in schools. They are presented as guidelines, or standards that are somewhat flexible, since, as discussed in Chapter 1, the school counseling situation is less formal and structured than the professional one.

First, the neutrality principle implies that a teacher should refrain from giving advice. (The distinctions between counseling and advising are discussed at length in Chapter 1.) Second, it suggests that the teacher should be mindful of his or her uses of personal disclosure. By this we mean, for example, that before a teacher tells a student about having faced the same problem in school, he or she must decide whether this fact will be useful to the student or whether drawing parallels between their experiences is assuming too much and possibly confusing the student's story with the teacher's.

Third, the neutrality principle requires that the teacher's personal reaction to the student's situation does not overlap the student's to an excessive degree and thereby lead to the so-called "rescue fantasy" as well. Some people who come to us remind us of ourselves, or of the times in our lives when we felt afraid or helpless. The teacher's wish to rescue a student from a difficult situation often comes out of a frightening sense on the teacher's part of his or her own helplessness. To the extent that that fear is driving the teacher, he or she will be prevented from understanding the student's own situation and the student's ability to solve the problem.

The fourth—and probably most important—rule derived from the neutrality principle is that when there is a problem in a counseling relationship—when the student is not able to use the help the teacher is providing and continues to have difficulties—the teacher needs to consider whether he or she is in some way inadvertently contributing to those difficulties. The teacher must ask, "Am I getting in the way here? Is something I am feeling or doing preventing me from hearing the student? Are matters in my own life intruding on this relationship and making it difficult for me to understand and be of help?" When something of this kind is going on, the teacher should seek help with the counseling work from a consultant or supervisor.

Understanding the Transference

Both individuals in any two-person relationship are experiencing at an unconscious level feelings which have to do with other relationships in their lives. So, just as a counselor needs to attend to personal biases or underlying judgments of a student, so must he or she consider those feelings which the student may be having in return. Parallel with the teacher's questions about neutrality are questions about the student's feelings toward the teacher: "What do I mean to the student? What position do I occupy in his or her life?" These two sets of questions, about neutrality and about what is known in psychoanalytic terms as "transference," are the key to understanding the interpersonal field in the relationship.

Students bring all kinds of feelings to their relationships with their teachers. They want their approval. They fear their authority, although some do not show that they do. To some extent they assume that the teacher occupies the same space as a parent would. Students, however, also have an opportunity to see a teacher from a distance—something they rarely can do with their parents. Students may notice in the teacher a particular quality which they like and admire and which they do not see in their parents. The teacher's position in a student's life therefore is somewhere between the stereotyped adult/parent authority figure and someone having a special quality which the student is looking for in a relationship at this point.

Students select the person they confide in because of that special quality which they feel matches their need. That quality usually has something to do with a capacity to provide a kind of mirroring, a capacity to understand the student, and an admiring, appreciative way of responding to him or her. That quality is what my patient was referring to when she said, "There were always some teachers who noticed when I did well." It was not just that they noticed; they spoke of it with her. They encouraged her to express more of herself and then admired what she did.

Students who find this kind of mirroring relationship with a teacher will put the teacher on a pedestal. Intuitively that makes a certain amount of sense. In order for the admiration and the appreciation that the teacher provides really to count, that teacher has to be special: He or she has to be a little larger than life, represent an ideal in some way, and then live up to it. That is, of course, a lot to ask of anyone, and there are times when an idealized notion about the teacher, which the student needs in order to support the feeling of being cared about in a meaningful way, unravels. The question on the teacher's mind then is, "what happens if I let the student down?" If a teacher has come to represent an ideal to a student and is providing something he or she is not getting anywhere else, he or she may be tested at some point. It is useful for the teacher to consider this possibility if, all of a sudden, a student becomes angry, will not visit, and will not talk—in other words, when there is an impasse of some kind.

The transference feelings of the student usually lie in his or her unconscious, and it is not the job of the teacher to interpret these matters to the student or even necessarily to discuss them at all. It may be helpful, however, for the teacher to wonder if an idealized fantasy did exist for the student and whether something has occurred to interrupt or shatter that fantasy. Perhaps the teacher misunderstood something the student said. Perhaps the teacher arrived late or forgot an appointment. Maybe the student learned something about the teacher's personal life which was somehow disappointing. It could be anything.

It is gratifying to a teacher to be idealized by a student and it is a problem, too, because no one can live up to idealized expectations all the time. So, while it is not wise to deflect fantasies in students all the time by reminding them that one is only human, it is important to be understanding of the role these feelings play in the relationship. That is what "understanding the transference" means. There is an opportunity in this close personal relationship between teacher and student for development of an image of the teacher—a sense, a persona that may or may not correspond with what the teacher really is. That person is usually a mix of people in the student's life and other relationships which responds to a need and fills the gap that other relationships do not fill.

Looking at neutrality and transference together, then, we see that in the counseling situation there are at least four people in the room: two real people and two imaginary ones. The imaginary ones shift, change, and come in and out of focus with the real ones. Often we cannot tell which we are in the other's eyes, and we are surprised when we are confronted by a sense that we are not to them who we think we are.

In some, these are complicated matters having to do with the interpersonal field in counseling—that is, what is happening between the two people involved that is not visible to the naked eye. This metarelationship—the one within the other, the one which we cannot plan or control—is at the heart of the counseling interaction. Usually we cannot entirely understand it or make it fit reality. Sometimes, though—particularly when the relationship is foundering—it is useful to wonder whether something has happened which we cannot objectively document to change the balance in the imagined relationship; some attention to that shift or change may be necessary before the real relationship can proceed.

The part of the relationship that the counselor or teacher can affect is in himself or herself. The teacher can look for the aspects in the relationship that are uncomfortable in some way. The teacher can ask, "Is it too close? Am I not getting the point? Am I trying to rush things? Is this a student I cannot like or admire or care very deeply about? Is this student too dependent on me? Am I always worried that I will let him down? Do I know things I wish I did not know?" If the teacher is anxious about the relationship, there is usually a good reason, but there is usually something that can be done to resolve the problem. The teacher must listen very attentively to himself or herself and to the student to know that there is a problem, and should if possible talk it over with a consultant or supervisor to decide on a way to resolve it.

The Problem of Confidentiality

As stated in Chapter 1, the informal counseling dialogue that occurs between students and teachers deserves the protection of confidentiality, just as any such conversation would if it occurred in a professional office. Teachers, however, are in a different position from the professional counselor; the expectations of them are different, since they are accountable to the school administration as well as to the student and to the student's parents. Communication between a student and a teacher is not legally privileged. Accordingly, the boundries of the relationship—what is permitted to go *out* in the way of information about the student—are, ultimately, whatever the teacher decides they are. The teacher's decisions about those boundaries are influenced by school policy, by the climate in the school, and by the teacher's own feelings.

Confidentiality can be a big problem in the small world of an independent school, where it is not uncommon for everyone to know everyone else's business—or feel they are entitled to know it. Word, and sometimes gossip, travels fast in communities in which people know each other and are involved in the close ways teachers are with students and colleagues.

In some schools, teachers are also expected, either explicitly or implicitly, to report to an administrator anything of an important personal nature which a student tells them. This expectation often conflicts with a school's efforts to encourage the development of trust between students and teachers, so teachers find themselves with the choice of risking their jobs or risking their relationship with a student. That choice is stressful for the teacher, and it is not one the teacher can continue to make in the long run.

The two questions here are: First, how does the teacher protect boundaries in a relationship with a student and provide confidentiality in the small community of the school? Second, when is it not appropriate to keep secrets? When is it necessary to get help from the community by involving someone else in the counseling dialogue? Addressing these questions will, hopefully, help to clarify the tension the teacher may feel about confidentiality and lead to a way for schools to address the problem.

The bottom line in this matter is that students will not speak freely about personal issues if there is any doubt in their minds that what they say will be treated respectfully. Students simply do not talk to people they do not trust. For counseling to go on in a school, there must be a *policy* and a *climate* which provide opportunities for students to build trust in the adults around them. If the school rigidly requires teachers to report what they hear to the administration, or if the atmosphere is such that things just get around, there will be no counseling to speak of, and there will be a lot of secrets among the students.

But sometimes students say, "You have to promise not to tell anybody what I'm about to tell you." The fact that they are about to tell a teacher something important already means that they trust that person. Without realizing it, however, they are putting the teacher in a bind. The teacher worries, "what if I have to tell someone? What if I cannot handle this alone?"

The job for the teacher is to translate this demand into something he or she can work with. In most instances this demand is an expression of certain feelings in the student: (1) the student's feeling of urgency that the matter be addressed privately and not spoken of around the school, (2) the student's fear that other adults will misunderstand and react negatively in some ways to what he or she is experiencing, (3) a feeling of trust that the teacher has a special ability to help out at this moment, and (4) a desire on the student's part to be in control of what happens to the information and the wish that the teacher respect that desire. If the teacher bears all of these feelings in mind and addresses the student's concerns, he or she will be able to preserve confidentiality and act responsibly as well. The teacher needs to create a channel for *safe passage* of personal matters.

Even in schools in which the administration grants teachers complete discretionary authority to handle issues confidentially, problems sometimes occur. Let us imagine a situation in which a teacher must report what he or she has heard—for example, a serious health problem. The teacher's first obligation is to tell the student what he or she has to do and take responsibility for his or her actions. The teacher should refrain from saying, "This is for your own good," and instead say, "I feel I have a responsibility here, and this is the decision I have to make." Then the teacher should try to include the student in planning how to proceed. The teacher might ask, "Can you and I talk about how to handle this together? Can we talk about how to tell your parents (or the dean or the school consultant) what you have told me? I will help you do it, but we need to talk together and think about it first. I know it will be hard to do, but I think it has to be this way."

There will be times when this course is unacceptable to the student and when the student feels that the teacher is betraying a trust. But if the teacher has used good judgment and been respectful of the student, there is a very good chance the relationship will survive in the long run. After a crisis has been handled carefully, the student usually realizes that something has been gained.

The matter of confidentiality—how personal information is handled—is an educational issue in the school. Children keep secrets, and they make each other swear to keep secrets. When they are angry at each other, they often blackmail each other with secrets or betray a trust. Adults, on the other hand, should be able to keep a secret, but they also must know when they need help to solve a problem. They have to earn people's trust by respecting what they hear in confidence, but they also must live up to their responsibilities in the community. There is a developmental process involved in moving from the child's position to the adult's. In a community in which children and adults mingle as closely as they do in a school, these matters are always being negotiated.

Confidentiality—the climate of respect—in a school deserves at least as much in the way of periodic review as the budget or the curriculum. One set of questions is: "Do the students trust the teachers? Do the teachers trust the administration? Does the administration trust the teachers?" In a school in which the answer to any of those three questions is negative, there will exist a serious morale problem and there will be problems in any counseling program that is developed.

There are also questions to be asked concerning the counseling relationships that do exist between students and teachers: "Is there enough respect between student and teacher for them to handle a difficult decision about confidentiality together? Is there some way that facing such a decision and resolving the problem together can help both to grow and learn something they had not understood before? Does the administration have enough confidence in the faculty and the students to let this process unfold privately and, at the same time, be available supportively if the need arises?"

In the final analysis, confidentiality is a matter of respect and trust among all the members of the community, and ongoing review and concern is necessary at all levels. Rules and official policy are not a substitute for real commitment to that respect and trust, nor do they by themselves offer true guidelines for teachers or students. The school as a whole needs to come to some shared set of guidelines and expectations and to examine, evaluate, and be prepared to amend those periodically.

Termination

When a close counseling relationship has developed over time between teacher and student, it is sometimes difficult to bring it to an end. Termination is an important part of the counseling experience, but—again, because of the informal structure of the counseling relationships in schools—it is often not understood well or dealt with fully. The word itself is a little misleading, too. Meaningful relationships do not abruptly "terminate." They close, they recede, they move into the past, and they exist as a part of ourselves in some way for the rest of our lives.

So, what does the teacher do at that arbitrary point at which one should say good-by? How does one decide that time has arrived? How does one acknowledge how much the relationship has meant and still let go? Is there a way to define the moment of termination and to help someone let go and move away, taking some part of the relationship with them? Sometimes the teacher has no control over the timing of the termination. A student may just leave without explanation, then find reasons not to resume counseling. Most often, the school year ends and the student goes away for the summer. By fall, he or she seems different, is not so involved with the counselor, and is not inclined to take up the counseling work again. Seniors graduate and go to college, and do not write or come back as they promised to do.

As people grow and change they have mixed feelings about the relationships they leave behind. On the one hand, they know that they will miss the warmth and protection of the early relationships with parents or supportive adults they have known along the way. On the other hand, they feel excited about the new experiences they are having and do not want to feel encumbered by old ties. The first group of feelings—the sadness and the longing to stay close—are the more hidden in most people.

Every person has his or her own characteristic way of passing through channels of transition and of navigating the experience of loss. Such times can be intense, and there is for many people a need to maintain control, to not give in to the feelings of upheaval that are just under the surface. Some people feel, "If I give in to the feelings of sadness and loss, will I be able to recover and go on?" Much of the time, when it comes to loss, people say to themselves—as Scarlet says in *Gone With the Wind*—"I'll think about that tomorrow." By the time tomorrow comes, the loss is over and in the past, stored in memory but denied access to feeling.

As a technical matter in counseling, we are not advocating long, drawn-out sentimental good-bys as the way to effect termination. Not every bit of the relationship has to be recapitulated, felt, or acknowledged for there to be closure. There is, however, a need to talk about the mixture of feelings. The reason is that, as people go on in life, losses that are left unacknowledged remain with them like ghosts, haunting new relationships, leaving them confused about their feelings for people, somewhat doubting about relationships, and a little disabled at handling losses later.

The task for the counselor, as we suggested earlier, is to talk with the student about the ending of the relationship and, in the process, give the student something to take along. Sometimes a present is appropriate—something of the teacher's that the student can keep, that will remind the student of the relationship, and that, in giving it, makes the teacher feel he or she has moved on with the student. A present is a very concrete way to preserve the relationship through the changes in the student's life and to say "good-by" at the same time.

More often though, the gift at parting can just as well be some simple words. For example, the teacher can say, "I feel proud and hopeful for you." "I feel as though I have seen you grow." "I'm glad I was here when you needed help." "I'll miss you." "Write or stop by. It will always be important to me to know how you're doing." Such words help to define the relationship and cast it in such a way that a sense of its meaning forms and can last.

The difficulties which teachers or counselors have had in dealing with losses in their own lives—the ghosts of unresolved relationships in their own pasts—make it hard for them sometimes to know when to let go. Everyone has some feeling of unfinished business in relationships which can make it difficult to see when something *should* finish. How does the teacher know when the time has come?

The easiest way to tell is to notice when things are better in the student's life. Students seek help from teachers when they are having trouble in a number of areas in their lives. By the time they have done the work of understanding their difficulties, there has usually been some improvement in the circumstances in their lives as well as in their self-esteem. General improvement of this kind is an indication that the counseling work can be terminated.

Students tell teachers in indirect ways that they want to move on. They become involved in new relationships. Sometimes they forget appointments because they are not as involved with talking about their difficulties as they are in living out some of the solutions they have discovered. Sometimes, too, students forget appointments because they know they are reaching the end of the counseling relationship and are nervous about talking about termination with the teacher.

It is sometimes hard for the teacher to keep in mind that students are *supposed* to be leaving. There is a natural developmental force in adolescents urging them on, urging them away. There is in some adults a natural force in the other direction, making them want to pull in, consolidate, make lasting commitments. Adults can be somewhat resistant to change, particularly when losses in their own lives have been unacknowledged or unresolved. Such feelings were hidden in a role play done at a workshop at an independent school a number of years ago. The teacher and the student had worked together over a period of time and had come to a good resolution of some difficult matters in the student's life. The relationship had been of real value to both of them. The student went away for vacation. When she returned, the teacher met her at the train. She looked at him and said, "What are you doing here?" Both people were caught off guard, having not acknowledged that the vacation marked a natural endpoint of the counseling relationship. Both were embarrassed. The student was a little angry; the teacher was a little hurt.

Mistakes such as this are probably inevitable, and they are definitely forgivable as a natural occurrence in the complex, subtle give-and-take of human relationships. The only lesson in the story is in the vulnerability of the teacher, who may fail on occasion to notice his or her own avoidance of feelings about loss, sometimes at the expense of an important piece of the counseling work.

Conclusion

To my knowledge, none of these technical, interpersonal matters were ever taken up between my patient and her teachers—the ones who noticed when she did well. They talked, but the teacher's neutrality was probably not considered to be much of an issue. Her teachers were probably not aware of how much she idealized them or how much she feared their judgment of her. They had no idea, I am sure, of the deficits in her family relationships which they helped her overcome. Confidentiality was not a pressing matter because she did not reveal very much of her deeper personal concerns. It is unlikely that anyone ever spoke of termination, because it simply was a fact of life—a matter of course in the relationships between teachers and students.

For the most part, teachers do not need to worry about these technical matters in their relationships with students. Teachers help students primarily by being themselves, by being available and open, and by being able to see the unique value in the person inside the student.

The unifying lesson in this discussion of technical problems in counseling, however, concerns the importance of *self-knowledge* in the teacher. In the long run, the skill developed in the teacher-counselor grows in that medium, in the capacity to reach inward and bring the best of oneself to the relationship in a way that is both open and knowing. Technique in the counselor starts in the awareness that one has an effect on the student at every moment, and that at every moment the student has an effect on the counselor. There are bound to be snags and problems in the process, which can probably be resolved by considering one or more of the technical issues discussed in this chapter. Beyond that, though, is the all-important need on the counselor's part to listen to himself or herself. The work of counseling requires this effort of us and, at the same time, deepens our awareness of ourselves with every new relationship we encounter.

Chapter 10

RECOGNIZING RED FLAGS

Preston K. Munter

Everyone knows the meaning of red and green traffic signals and exactly how to react to them. When the conductor of an orchestra raps his baton on the music stand, we know that the concert is about to begin. At the Kennedy Space Center, a countdown precedes the launching of a space vehicle. At the Metropolitan Opera House in New York City, those famous chandeliers rise to the ceiling to signal the beginning of the performance. All of these symbolic events signal action that is about to take place. Within the cultural or a social context, everyone understands the meaning of such signals and reacts accordingly.

So it is with what we call "red flags" in the behavior of students. They are signals that people are in trouble, and they should trigger appropriate responses on the part of teacher-counselors. Unfortunately, the meanings of these red flags are not always as clear as those of a traffic light, and they do not always indicate precisely what one's reactions should be. Indeed, the basic challenge for teacher-counselors is to be able to identify danger signs in people and in the circumstances of a school community. Signals often indicate that something is going to happen when, by the very nature of the circumstances, it is not possible to know exactly what. It is the nagging anxiety of the unknown that is so troublesome, especially when we somehow sense that the impending event may be intrinsically threatening or actually dangerous and that if we only *knew* what it was, we might be able to take measures to avoid it. Unfortunately, we are not

157

likely to know precisely what it is that is going to happen, who will be involved, when it is going to occur, or how and why it will happen. Without that knowledge, our only recourse is to bring whatever experience and intuition we possess to bear and, observing such cues as there are and to make a reasonable judgment about what to do— if anything.

This chapter discusses the red flags in students' behavior and, to a lesser extent, in school situations to which teacher-counselors should pay special attention. We will also consider some actions which may be prompted by such signals. Our purpose here is not, however, to provide a complete catalogue of signals and responses. Rather we wish to heighten teacher-counselor awareness of emergency situations and help *prepare* them to deal with the problems. Certain specific suggestions and advice will be given, some applicable to a given school situation or individual. Above all, we wish to encourage counselors to identify specific red flags in their own situations *before* trouble appears, so that they can take measures to avoid the trouble. Specifically what to do and how to do it is best and most effectively learned by hands-on activity and experience.

There is a basic lesson for those charged with the responsibility of dealing with emergencies or those who simply by chance find themselves in an emergency situation: In order to recognize the meaning of red flags and react to them in an appropriate manner, it is absolutely essential to be prepared for the unexpected, the surprising, the shocking. It is also necessary to prepare oneself to understand the real meaning of something so obvious that we are likely to make wrong assumptions. A red flag may, indeed, turn out to have a different significance in present circumstances than it has in the past and, therefore, requires special consideration.

In this connection, it is important for teacher-counselors to have specific knowledge of what the climate or atmosphere—even the culture—of their school is like ordinarily—that is, what the operational baseline is, so to speak, on a normal day. The normative level of functioning of the school provides a reference point for calibrating the significance of events which appear to be unusual. In general, schools and students engage in a process of accommodation with one another in which the growth of the individual takes place in harmony with the growth of other individuals and with the welfare of the community. Anything that disrupts this balance may be a warning.

The Teacher's Untapped Knowledge of Red Flags

Experience over the years at the Institutes and elsewhere has made it abundantly clear from a counseling point of view that teachers have a deep and largely untapped reservoir of knowledge about adolescents. That fact is surely no surprise. Nevertheless teachers seem to have difficulty believing that their experience is applicable to counseling troubled students. At the Institutes, one of our continuing tasks has been to persuade teachers of the specific relevance of their classroom experience to counseling and to help them mine that experience for the lode of knowledge embedded in it. We encourage them to make use of *all* of their experience in counseling their students. Because most secondary school teachers are in direct and indirect contact with students for many hours each day, their ample store of information about students can amplify their counseling skills, especially in identifying red flags, to a significant extent if properly explored, understood, and utilized.

Thus, a primary aim of the Institutes is to make it clear to teachers that they are actually more able to recognize students who are in difficulty than they are aware of or willing to acknowledge. Understandably, teachers may feel the need to augment the knowledge and skills they already have in hand or to prepare themselves in more particular ways to deal with troubled students. Whatever their perceived needs may be in this regard—and they are likely to vary from one teacher to another—they can be met with relative ease and in a relatively short time. At Northfield and Fountain Valley we have observed repeatedly that, with relatively modest effort, teachers—in all subject areas—can learn quite readily much of what they need to know to be effective and appropriate counselors. Furthermore, if they are willing to draw on their experience in the classroom, they can become not only remarkably helpful counselors but also sophisticated monitors of urgent or emergency situations in short order.

As pointed out in Chapters 2 and 5, however, teachers are frequently and unnecessarily reluctant to counsel students who have what might be called the normative problems of adolescence on the grounds that they do not have the knowledge or experience to do so. Furthermore, they commonly feel that even if they do have the knowledge, to intervene as a counselor would somehow be intrusive. Another goal of the Institutes, therefore, has been not only to heighten teachers' awareness of the level of sophistication their experience has already given them but to authenticate their use of it in counseling. Like all basic lessons, these must be endlessly rehearsed even by veteran counselors because, among several reasons, it helps everyone manage the anxieties generated by the risk-taking business of counseling so vividly exemplified when teachers find themselves confronting red flag circumstances.

And, counseling students does have its risks, for professional therapists as well as for teacher-counselors. But the risks can be minimized in a number of ways. First and foremost it is essential to remain oneself—that is, to use one's personal style honestly and directly rather than trying to adopt a "therapeutic manner." Indeed, being oneself as honestly and openly as possible is a hallmark of any competent counselor. Another major way for teacher-counselors to minimize their risks is to prepare themselves as well as possible for the unexpected. And that is, fundamentally, what this chapter is about: preparedness; *awareness* and preparedness.

Being aware and prepared does not, however, have to mean being obsessively worried about every possible meaning of each slightly unusual behavior. It does mean that teacher-counselors who understand the complexity and variety of the clues to trouble that exist in every school community should pay attention when something suggestive appears on their horizon. People who are aware and responsive make a school community considerably more sophisticated and, to a real extent, immeasurably safer and better equipped to deal with problems as they arise.

Teachers' Anxiety about Failing to Recognize Trouble

Teachers are understandably concerned about failing to recognize that a student may be getting into serious trouble. Quite naturally, they worry about not being able to react effectively and in a timely fashion. The classic example of this situation is anxiety about not being able to prevent a student from attempting suicide. Suicide is a matter of the gravest concern to everyone who works in a school, especially those teachers who function as counselors. At the Institutes, we have learned that teachers can realistically expect to reduce or limit the risk of student suicide. At the same time it is well to bear in mind that even the most seasoned professional cannot guarantee to avoid all the pitfalls of counseling, much less all of the risks—major and minor—that are inherent in it.

Virtually all participants come to the Institutes with a built-in defense against allowing themselves to "get in too deeply." They are armed with a sharp awareness—indeed a sensitivity—that almost automatically protects them from taking on a counselee who is frankly ill or in some other respect beyond their counseling skills. That sensitivity is valuable as well as understandable, even though it makes teachers especially reactive when they think they have failed to recognize that a given student was more troubled than was readily apparent, or that there was an urgent or emergent situation which, without adequate warning, required their intervention.

Preparing to Handle Emergencies

There is a great deal that teachers can do to prepare themselves to deal with red flag situations. They can maintain a constant high level of awareness of the possibilities by elaborating and extending their repertoire of the signs and signals given by people who are in significant difficulty. Awareness and knowledge are components of a cognitive process, in the course of which they can prepare themselves to react more or less spontaneously and in timely fashion when actually faced with an emergency situation. The overall process includes the following seven components or stages:

1. Informing oneself of the various kinds of red flags and learning as much as possible about the nature and range of signs of trouble that students can manifest either outwardly or subtly.
2. Learning to recognize the possibilities of difficulty in given situations.
3. Assessing the likelihood of the existence of an emergency based upon what is unknown as well as what is known.
4. Assessing the risks that appear to be inherent in any given situation.
5. Making the decision to act (or not).
6. Deciding what action to take and how to take it.
7. Taking certain specific actions, such as referral to an outside professional.

This process can be set in motion in considerably less time than it takes to read about it, provided the prior stage is in place on a continuing basis—namely, that the counselor keeps himself or herself in a state of readiness. In this sense, being properly prepared is the result of training oneself to be constantly aware of the *possibility* that trouble may come in many guises, together with the simple willingness to consider "ordinary" events as possibly having more than ordinary significance. It is necessary to be sufficiently sensitive in this regard as to be able to differentiate the malign from the benign character of events.

As previously indicated, while one need not be in a perpetual state of hyperawareness and reactivity, some stance of preparedness is basic for counselors. Overall it is one of the most useful tools for all counselors, just as it is for all therapists. There is no question that even the most seasoned professionals find it necessary to refine and expand their knowledge of these matters and sharpen their awareness of them on a continuing basis throughout their careers. Even though one can become more and more adept at recognizing the signs of potential trouble, probably no one ever completely masters the skill, or art, of doing so. There is always more to learn, more to add to one's repertoire, more to understand about one's own reactions to the threat of trouble. That is partly because each troublesome situation is likely to have an individuated character and each troubled individual a distinct mode of expressing trouble.

To a large extent, the singularity of emergency situations is also due to the anxiety and tension felt by everyone in the face of the unknowns that almost invariably encumber the awareness that trouble is brewing. The urge to deny the situation, the wish to avoid it, the fear of confronting it, and the uncertainty common to these situations only further complicate the matter. All of these factors inevitably make us react in ways that may vary markedly from situation to situation. Lastly, emergency situations are rarely presented as simple reality but, rather, as a complex of conflicting and confusing circumstances. "When fortunes come, they come not single spies but in battalions," as the Bard tells us.

It requires some study, a good bit of work, and a fair amount of hands-on experience to develop any of the capacities or skills necessary to be well prepared to handle emergencies. By any measure, the easiest to develop is a body of information about the kinds of difficulties that students and school communities may present. Primarily this is a rather straightforward learning process. Let us now discuss each stage of the process previously outlined.

Informing Oneself about the Sources, Nature and Range of Signs of Trouble

Warnings of trouble come from any number of sources in and around a school. In general, the most common clues are given by students themselves, and they will be discussed in some detail. But first, let us consider some sources of warnings outside the school, for red flags appear outside the school community as well as inside.

Teachers need to be aware of the potential impact on the school climate of trouble and tension in the larger community beyond the school. Parents, members of the board of education or school committee, or other people with a vested interest in a school all may react in ways indicating that some sort of difficulty is developing. In addition, social, political, and economic unrest are likely to be reflected in the school community, provoking both individual and school-wide reactions. These may be directly related to outside disturbances—for example, the 1960s demonstrations—or to latent and apparently unrelated problems which, although close to the surface, do not become visible or audible until triggered by these additional pressures. And military "adventures" are almost by definition cues for reaction in a student body, especially one composed of adolescents and young adults in whom idealism and anti-authoritarianism lie close to the surface and in whom a sense of moral outrage is so readily provoked.

The red flags of situational difficulties that occur within the school community are all too familiar to teachers: troubled faculty-student relationships, troubled relationships within the faculty and between faculty and administrators, financial pressures, and the whole range of pressures exerted on schools from the outside, particularly those relating to college advisers, curricula, "standards," and "values." And, of course, there is the sometimes intrusive behavior of over-solicitous (vs. appropriately concerned) parents as a possible herald of trouble in their children.

Student group activity characteristic of adolescents and young adults (especially in their "social" activity) and the conduct of key students in school life often presage problems for individual students as well as for the school community. A "ringleader," such as a recalcitrant editor of the school newspaper with a special axe to grind or a perpetrator of practical jokes, are surely people to pay special attention to. In the 1960s groups of students acted in a highly disruptive and sometimes destructive manner in order to express their concerns about public affairs of one kind or another, notably the Vietnam war. There were many warning signs that preceded such outbreaks, although at the time many people erroneously thought that they occurred without any warning at all. We tend to think of that kind of red flag as a thing of the past, but students are always inclined to public protests. Teachers should not be caught off guard by events similar to those of the 1960s on campuses and in schools. The Saturday night beer-bust and the post-football game "coke" party are two examples of students sending signs of more generalized trouble. Such behavior must be recognized for what it means beyond the immediate trouble it causes and an appropriate response must be made.

When an individual member of the faculty or administration becomes upset in some way (it is always noticeable to students) or is accused of guilt or wrongdoing, such circumstances should be understood to have red flag significance. It is more than likely that there will be a reaction in the school community, usually among students, and the faculty and administration should be prepared for it.

For the most part, competent teachers recognize the kinds of behavior in individual students that plainly indicate the presence or onset of trouble. Among those behaviors are persistent acting up; repetitive or extreme acting out, such as lying, cheating, stealing, and destructive or threatening acts or other behavioral evidences of irresponsibility; cruelty and insensitivity to peers; disregard of the accepted limits within the school community, such as unusual rebelliousness; abuse of alcohol and prescription drugs, hallucinogens, stimulants, depressants, and the whole contemporary inventory of substances so inappropriately and inexactly named "recreational" drugs; accident proneness; disordered eating patterns; and—probably of most importance—the classic behavioral evidence of personal difficulty among students, namely, an apparently inexplicable deterioration in academic performance in otherwise perfectly able students.

As has already been pointed out, how individual students behave, react and, most importantly, feel is key to a focal group of red flags. Physiological disturbance or dysfunction represents one subset, so to speak, of these red flags. They are of special significance because they are more readily accessible than most. But faculty members are not so likely to be aware of them, partly because they are troublesome enough in and of themselves and partly because they feel that their inquiry into physiological matters is restricted by social convention or a sense of delicacy which, though quite appropriate in usual social circumstances, is clearly to be set aside in an emergency situation. In any case, physiological dysfunction is often a signal of more generalized and profound difficulty and sometimes in students is the *only* observable precursor of it. In most circumstances, information about such problems is easily elicited merely by directly questioning students. Among such disturbances are weight gain and loss, disturbed sleep, abnormal bowel and appetite patterns, skin disturbances, and, notably, students' persistent and repetitive complaints about physical discomfort or disability in the absence of confirming medical data.

The major cluster of red flags which identify individuals who are developing major difficulties or who may already be seriously compromised are those in the realm of emotions and interpersonal relationships. These signals are less easily identified and their significance with regard to emergencies is sometimes more difficult to understand. Teacher-counselors are well advised to learn to recognize these signals, for the rewards in the form of diminished anxiety are very real. Among these red flags are uncharacteristically odd or even bizarre behavior such as withdrawal from usual social and personal relationships; extreme seclusiveness; apathy or enervated mental and physical activity, on the one hand, or notably pressured mental and physical activity on the other; anxiety, tension, stress or obvious sadness; and self-destructiveness—whether behavioral or "only" ideational.

Self-destructiveness is *always* serious. It can occur in a range of seriousness from suicidal ideas, to overt threats of suicide, to suicidal gestures, and, finally, to overt suicide attempts. These forms of self-destruction can usually be differentiated. From the point of view of assessing the risk to the involved student, such differentiation is essential. While on the face of it, a suicide attempt is likely to be a significantly greater threat to life than a passing suicidal idea, it is clear that one cannot be absolutely sanguine about how valid, precise, or dependable such differentiation can be within any particular student. Indeed, the potential lethality of a particular form of suicidal reaction is specifically what one must appreciate and evaluate.

Other red flags which signal serious emotional difficulties are deteriorated interpersonal relationships; marked decline in academic performance and fulfillment of responsibilities; patterned social or antisocial behavior; and, of prime importance, a student's communication, directly or indirectly, that he or she is seriously troubled, *regardless* of all other evidence, including readily observable but perhaps unremarkable social and interpersonal behavior and academic and extracurricular performance. More specific and detailed description of such student difficulties and their particular significance as red flags is outside the purpose of this chapter, but the experience of the Institutes is clear: Relatively modest sensitivity to the existence of such red flags and of the possibilities of trouble inherent in them can help teacher-counselors become considerably better prepared to deal with students who develop or threaten to develop significant problems. Beyond that, teachers who are willing to expend rather minimal effort to learn more about them, not to mention becoming truly sophisticated about such matters, can become a solid and dependable resource in the school community as members of the counseling staff.

It is not often the teacher's task to become the ongoing counselor after an emergency situation has ended. Instead the teacher-counselor, recognizing such red flags, will be in an advantageous position to guide the troubled student to appropriate helping resources, usually outside the school. Teachers have expressed their need for developing all these capacities and skills quite clearly at the Institutes. The most common question at Northfield and at Fountain Valley is, "What do you do when?"

Learning to Recognize the Possibilities of Difficulty in a Given Situation

Being prepared means more than remembering any catalogue of specifics, useful though that may be from time to time. Of more importance, though not so easy to achieve, is a general awareness, *a sense* of impending trouble in any given set of circumstances, even though one cannot be entirely rational about the feeling and cannot, through linear reasoning, articulate the nature of the trouble. It is, if you will, a kind of street smarts, a talent which some people seem to have naturally but which most of us need to work at in order to develop.

Some people seem never to develop such a sensitivity and are almost invariably caught off guard by some red flag situation or other. Despite their ability to recite a whole litany of circumstantial, behavioral, physiological, and psychological possibilities, they are always unprepared. It is as though such people are not sufficiently aware of the cues that are there or, being aware of them, either do not read them accurately or in their anxiety deny their meaning, and therefore do not "feel" the threat or danger. In such cases, teachers are, as it were, cue-neutral, or cue-immune, or cue-inert. Obviously, this condition is not sinful, wicked, criminal, or willfully irresponsible or mischievous. Yet one of the enduring lessons of the Institutes is that those teachers who are unaware and nonreactive in this way are probably not in the best position to handle emergencies. They should recognize this reality and so should their colleagues, administrators, headmasters, or principals. Nor are such teachers as likely to be effective counselors as they might otherwise be. More or less the same cue-sensitivity that makes it possible for counselors to listen effectively is required to gather the sort of data that makes for preparing oneself to handle emergencies and to respond to them expeditiously.

Assessing the Likelihood of an Emergency Based upon What Is Unknown as Well as What Is Known

The third step in the process of preparing oneself to be an effective overseer, so to speak, of the integrity of students and of the school community is to assess the likelihood that a problem of some sort may exist. What relevant information is known? Reports of declining academic performance by a student's math teacher? A football coach's concern that his star quarterback seems to have forgotten how to engineer carefully rehearsed and staged plays on the field? A dorm master's observation that a young woman, who does not seem to be eating much lately, has begun to show a noticeable degree of weight loss? What is *unknown* about these three students that, if known, might help clarify whether or not any of them has a serious problem?

In the first case, what possible explanations could there be for the student's academic slide? Trouble at home? "Significant other" problems? Inappropriate choice of courses? A poor relationship with a teacher? Problems in other courses? A telling blow—from what source?—to his or her self-esteem? Anything else, such as drugs or alcohol? Possibly just the usual adolescent unrest? Maybe more information—and more possibilities—need to be brought into the picture, but which ones? Where and how should the teacher-counselor look for them?

In the case of the quarterback, has something happened between him and his teammates? Or between him and the coach? What about trouble at home? Or some physical problem or illness? Or a significant loss—psychologically, intellectually, or socially? Another case of injured self-esteem? Could this be his way of giving up quarterbacking, or football altogether? Why would he do that? Does he show signs of "forgetting" or confusion in the classroom? Maybe the coach should ask him about some of these possibilities instead of just chewing him out? Or merely ask him how he feels to see where that leads? Could it be that he has simply lost his zest for the game? If so, why? Anything else? Drugs? No, not this guy—a star athlete and all-American boy type. But could that be? Again, the unknowns seem to stretch on and on.

As for the young woman who is losing weight, has anyone noticed that she has been ill lately? On the contrary she is as lively and energetic as ever—if not more so. Can you be ill and still be so energized? Is it possible that the school nurse or physician knows anything? If so, can the information be shared? If not, then what? Is the weight loss very marked? How does she seem otherwise? Any other losses—academically or socially? Other likely explanations? It would be helpful to know if she is behaving the same way at mealtimes at home. How to find out? Again—lots of possibilities. In the end, however, more remains unknown than known about the student and her problem, if, indeed, she actually has one. So how is it possible to proceed?

Assessing the Risks That Appear to Be Inherent in Any Given Situation

In each case, the next step in preparing oneself for possible intervention is to assess the risks inherent in the particular situation. Given all the options, what *are* the possible risks? One way to determine that is to consider the worst-case scenario in each instance. Among the individuals described above, for example, is the first student so badly off that he might flunk out altogether? If so, does that mean his motivation or ability is gravely compromised? The trouble may be coming from somewhere on the outside and therefore will be difficult or impossible to identify. If that is the case, will the student flunk out without receiving the help that might facilitate an attempt on his part to reverse that fate? What if the quarterback messes things up in the key game two weeks hence? Is he that badly off? And if he is and does, will he not be in a really difficult situation in his relationship with his peers? And, if that happens, how will he react? Will he take off for home or somewhere else—or try something worse, perhaps something self-destructive, especially if there is the additional possibility of a recent telling wound to his self-esteem? And if our young woman with the apparent weight problem continues losing weight much longer, she may develop serious physiological problems. How serious could they be? After all, people do die of extreme weight loss and its accompanying metabolic complications. How long is it safe to wait in order to test this premise? If she does lose much weight, should she leave school? Perhaps be treated in a hospital?

Are the risks in each of these situations at all similar? If not, how different are they? Which student seems to be at greatest risk? Which the least?

Making the Decision to Act, or Not

The next step in preparing oneself for an emergency is to decide whether action is called for. In each—or any—of the forgoing situations, is action called for *now*? If so, what should be done?

First of all is the basic problem of deciding that the information at hand—whether facts or objective data, limited or extensive, conflicting or confusing—indicates that *some* action is called for. In some instances the only information at hand may be the feelings or instincts of the teacher-counselor, however nonspecific, nonconfirmatory and devoid of persuasive data. The persistent concern, worry, anxiety, or puzzlement of an interested and caring teacher is quite likely the most significant red flag of all. Indeed, as already noted, that may be the only "fact" available in any given situation. Just as students' feelings must be understood as facts in the counseling process itself, so the sense or instinct of the teacher-counselor that a student is in trouble must be considered in a potential emergency.

Secondary school teachers have a good deal of experience with students in a variety of situations and circumstances: in the classroom, in the corridors, in the dining room, on the playing fields, and in various extracurricular activities. Their instinct, hunch, or feeling that a student seems to be headed for some kind of trouble may be more dependable as a basis for making a decision than almost any array of facts, reports, hearsay, and assorted messages from other faculty members or from the student's friends or family. It thus is well worth repeating and emphasizing that, in such cases, the teacher-counselor's feelings may be the facts of most significance. Indeed, it is perhaps not too much to say that, even in the face of contradictory "facts," a seasoned and experienced teacher-counselor is well advised to rely heavily on his or her own persistent anxieties about a potentially troubled student. This is likely to be true even though it may be difficult to define the cause of such anxieties in specific terms. Because the instincts of good teachers about their students are often more accurate indicators of what is happening, at least in a general sense, and more readily available than "hard data," they deserve very close attention as cues for decision making or action.

Deciding What Action to Take and How to Take It

Having recognized that the data at hand, whether in the form of objective or subjective information, indicate a decision to intervene, one must decide on the exact action to be taken—for example, seeking consultation in the form of another opinion, talking with someone in the administration, consulting the school nurse or physician, meeting with the student's family, or maybe undertaking crisis intervention counseling. Selecting from the possible alternatives is a judgment call that is almost entirely dependent upon the particular circumstances.

Whatever the decision, it should be implemented as definitively as possible but also compassionately. One should avoid being distracted by secondary concerns about administrative urgencies or other peripheral but essentially non-urgent matters. What this or that person's reaction might be to such action—even the reactions of the student himself or those of the student's family—should not interfere with the primary task of getting help for the student as expeditiously and appropriately as possible. In true emergencies, it may even be the case that the matter of confidentiality may have to be ignored or even knowingly breached in order to accomplish the primary task. Obviously if circumstances permit, there should be appropriate discussion with members of the student's family or the head of the school, thereby allowing for some sharing of the responsibility inher-

ent in almost all emergency situations. But in the absence of such indication, the concerned teacher will have to act alone. Hopefully, the
times when that will be both necessary and unavoidable will be rare.

All too often in an emergency, the teacher-counselor has difficulty
in deciding whether or not to take action because of the uncertainty
and ambivalence generated by his or her own anxiety or personal dilemma. The resulting delay can be a period of tension. The anxiety
that teachers commonly experience when trying to decide whether or
not to take action in an emergency situation is often because they
worry too much about the consequences of the decision. More often
than not, such consequences are essentially unpredictable with any
certainty and thus are largely indeterminate. To ask "What if—?" too
obsessively, as though *any* decision might carry with it really dire
consequences, is likely to obstruct the process of resolving the emergency and thereby to incur the possibility of precipitating greater
trouble than might have been inherent in the original situation.

In fact, acting rationally and decisively seldom brings on dire consequences. In those few situations in which the outcome is unfortunate, it is likely that almost any alternative course of action would not
have significantly changed the outcome. It is procedurally important
and immeasurably relieving for teachers to bear that reality in mind
when they are under the pressure of having to make such a decision.
At the least they will not be likely to find themselves so paralyzed by
their own intimations of disaster as to prevent them from intervening
in a way that is most likely to be helpful. And it is certainly worth
pausing once again over the fact that anyone, experienced or not, can
feel pressured and anxious in dealing with an emergency, sometimes
to a dysfunctional degree.

The heat and anxiety of finding oneself in a confusing and unclear
situation seems to *demand* responsible action which virtually guar-
antees to correct whatever is wrong, resolve the dilemma, prevent
the tragedy, or thwart a threatening danger. Most counselors feel considerably freer to act when they remember, realistically, how extremely rare it is that any one decision by an individual critically
alters the outcome for a troubled person. At best, such decisions can
only move a situation closer to resolution in one or two respects. Even
when there appears to be a clear threat of suicide, anyone who is
truly bent on self-destruction will likely be able to carry it out regardless of the intervention of a concerned teacher-counselor. In such
instances, intervention more than likely does nothing more than de-

lay the self-destructive behavior. On balance, however, it should be said that delay may provide the opportunity for other resources to be brought to bear. In some rare circumstances, that effort could be a great deal—perhaps, life-saving.

Generally speaking, it is important for teacher-counselors to remember that, in the emotional and behavioral realms, people have a somewhat limited repertoire of possible symptomatic behaviors which indicate that they may be threatened by serious trouble. Such manifestations are most likely to consist of patterns of reaction or behavior made up of disruption of the basic physiological, cognitive and emotional processes in combination with social or academic problems and interpersonal maladaptation, as already described. In addition, however, a cry for help on the part of an otherwise pained or terrified student should not be ignored or minimized, despite its obvious nature, and it should be as carefully assessed as circumstances permit.

It is worth noting that, despite their pain, students in severe personal difficulty may be skillful and purposeful in masking their difficulties. Thus the existence of a dysfunction in one sphere of experience—for example, severe disruption of sleep—may be only the lesser of two threatening evils. Against a more basic and threatening assault on self-esteem, such as the potential loss of a highly invested relationship, loss of some hours of sleep is not likely to be a serious matter. Insults to self-esteem, on the contrary, are much more threatening to adolescents and are, to a greater or lesser extent, almost always at risk in the emergency situations of young people.

Dealing with a Threat of Suicide

The specific actions teacher-counselors may take will depend, of course, on the particulars of the emergency situation in which they find themselves. In this connection, a student who is thought to be suicidal or one who is possibly suffering from a major emotional illness is of special concern. If the teacher-counselor's assessment is that suicide is a present danger, the counselor should remain with the student, *no matter what*, and immediately seek out appropriate help and support, whether from the school nurse or physician, the principal or headmaster, the student's family, the police, another faculty member, or even, all else failing, another student. This must be done without leaving the troubled student alone. It may therefore mean accompanying him or her to another place or office where such help is more readily available. The problem of students who are suicidal should be shared at all times. No individual teacher-counselor should attempt to manage that problem alone.

Students with Major Emotional Illness

In the case of the student who is thought to have a major emotional illness, once again appropriate help should be enlisted. In this case, the student's family should be notified and the student referred to an appropriate professional for evaluation. In making a referral to an outside resource such as a physician, for example, the teacher-counselor should be realistic, truthful, and practical, and, at the same time, compassionate. That means he or she should avoid making a diagnosis or telling the student that the referral is for treatment. Instead there should be a description of what has been observed in the student's behavior that led to the impression that outside intervention might be needed. It is not facilitating to say, for example, "I think you are schizophrenic." But it is likely to be useful to comment in some such fashion as, "You seem so sad and withdrawn, and even confused. And you say you have been unable to work. I am worried about you. I think it would be helpful to seek the advice of someone who understands these matters professionally. Dr. John Brown is the school's psychiatrist and he has been helpful to a number of students who have had such difficulties. We might ask him to help us evaluate your situation, too. Perhaps he will have some ideas as to how best to help you." It is preferable to identify the professional by name rather than as "a psychiatrist" or "a psychologist," or "a social worker."

Referral for Outside Help

It is of central importance that statements made to the student and the family be factual and that communication about the referral and the referral itself be accomplished in a straightforward manner. A student in this situation should *not* be referred to a physician for a disguised purpose or one that is misrepresented to the student. For example, it is not appropriate to tell the student that he is to have a regular physical exam, while telling the doctor privately to "check him out to see if he is having a nervous breakdown." The referral should be carried out in a benignly authoritarian manner, but with kindness and compassion. And the teacher-counselor should remain in the picture as the student's link to the routine school situation, at least until the outside evaluation is completed and appropriate measures to resolve the difficulty are in place.

Emergency Drill

Finally, each school should have an emergency routine for red flag situations, just as it has a fire drill. The structure and method of operation of such a procedure should be appropriate to the school situation. This is the last lesson of the Institute: the need for putting an organized, effective, understandable, manageable, and *rehearsed* system in place for handling emergency situations of the sort that have been discussed above. Unfortunately, it seems clear from what we have learned at the Institutes that many schools—perhaps most— do not have such a system in place. From the standpoint of meeting students' needs, its utility cannot be questioned, but its chief value lies beyond the pragmatics, important as they may be. The real value of an emergency system and drill is that both faculty and administration can take comfort from their knowledge that it exists and is in working order. That knowledge reduces the anxiety of faculty who are most likely to bear the brunt of dealing with emergency situations. It enables them to do so with infinitely greater efficiency than could be possible otherwise, and in that sense the entire school community can be reassured.

And so we end as we began, emphasizing the basic lesson about emergencies: Those who have the responsibility for handling such situations can be helped to become more effective. They also will be a good deal less anxious if they will take the trouble to prepare themselves thoroughly. That task is never completed, but is one which must be pursued, just as one's knowledge must be enlarged and one's experience amplified as long as one is involved in counseling matters.

As usual, Shakespeare said it all:

> *If your mind dislike anything, obey it. . . . We defy augury: there is a special providence in the fall of a sparrow. If it be now, 'tis not to come; if it be not to come, it will be now; if it be not now, yet it will come. The readiness is all.*

Chapter 11

THE STRUCTURE, PROCESS, AND GOALS OF THE INSTITUTE

Stanley H. King and Preston K. Munter

There have been many changes in the Institute since its beginning affecting the schedule, the composition of the faculty, the number of participants, and the program itself (which is overhauled annually). Most notably, the content of the lectures or topics to be discussed has changed a good deal over the past twenty-five years. The goals of the Institute, however, have not varied. From time to time, we may not have articulated them as clearly as now seems possible or desirable with the advantage of both reflection and hindsight. But in the most basic sense, the goals of the Institute remain the same for the 25th anniversary session at Northfield and the 5th anniversary session at Fountain Valley as they were for the very first Institute.

The fundamental goal is to help teachers develop, improve, and broaden their counseling skills. The process of the Institute, which takes place over seven days, is designed to achieve that goal. In accordance with their training and philosophy, the members of the faculty view the counseling process as a humanizing interaction between two people in the interest of problem solving and personal growth. They seek to make the process of the Institute reflect that view. In our opinion, counseling skills grow from that fundamental attitude; thus attitudes and skills are intertwined and inseparable. We aim to have the experience of the week's activities reflect the counseling process and to demonstrate what the basic ingredients of a counseling relationship are like. With that in mind, the process is oriented more toward the experiential than the didactic, enabling the participants to learn by doing, by feeling, and by interacting with the faculty and their peers. If we achieve something as basic at that, then how teachers counsel is technically of considerably less importance than that they counsel as they do—that is, in a compassionate, patient, supportive, and growth-inducing way. In the preceding chapters, this theme or major goal was examined in various aspects, giving the reader, we hope, some sense of what the seven days of the Institute are like.

Counseling encounters begin in many different ways. Some begin in the middle of things. Some start in a rather halting fashion, others with a flood of words and feelings. Some begin with a metaphor, or an inference, or a memory. Coming to understand what all of that may mean requires a sense of curiosity, a questioning attitude, the courage to wonder a little more about what may seem to be either perfectly obvious, clear, and understandable or utterly puzzling and incomprehensible—or even a bit of each. That sense of curiosity— part attitude, part skill—is crucial to the effective interaction between teacher and student. We seek to foster that curiosity from the first day, beginning with the discussion of the faculty role plays in front of all the participants. We wonder aloud, together, about how the teacher felt and what he or she observed in the body language and words of the student or of the counselor. We ask the participants to imagine themselves in the teacher-counselsor's chair, and we consider the differing reactions that people have, musing about what they might mean. We try very much to leave things open to question, to encourage exploration rather than arriving at closure. We hope participants understand that a sense of curiosity can be conveyed by the teacher to the student in the counseling interaction, that wondering about what is going on may be more important than fixing the problem at the moment. We try to keep the questioning attitude as alive as possible during the week. As the participants adopt it to understand themselves better as counselors, we try to help them see that what goes on in them reflects the counseling process and is an operative part of it.

Even though everyone shares much in the week together, it is likely that the Institute turns out to be a somewhat different experience for each participant. It is a week of many kinds of experiences, and each participant undoubtedly likes the flavor or feel of some better than others. We encourage everyone to try new experiences, even those they may think at first they will not like or "know" they will not like because they have already tried them. Some things just take getting used to: Role playing or counseling experiences often appear somewhat threatening at the beginning. We urge participants to give these new and different experiences a try and to see them as a necessary challenge to be overcome in order to grow not only as a counselor but personally as well.

It has been said, "Harmony in nature consists of an interplay of apparently conflicting forces." People often feel that there are puzzling dilemmas and paradoxes within themselves—even conflicting ones. Counseling is a way of helping them understand their particular paradoxes and conflicts so that they can achieve some harmony within themselves. Trying out new and different experiences may make people feel embarrassed or awkward, anxious or even exhilarated, but in such feelings they are likely to find greater understanding of themselves, and thus discover what is reflected in themselves, what takes place in the counseling interaction. This major goal requires a sense of curiosity, of exploration, of wondering; consequently it generates the special excitement that is so much a part of effective counseling.

Counseling encounters not only begin in many different ways, they also proceed in many different ways. Students as counselees may have as much difficulty with *how* to express themselves as they do with saying *what* it is that they have come to say. Some counseling dialogues go along fluently in what appears to be a rather structured, orderly way. More often they proceed in a series of apparently disconnected, even disparate phrases or statements or questions. Often a counseling dialogue consists of a series of statements that do not appear connected at first but that coalesce thematically as the counselor and student go along. There is a certain tolerance of ambiguity necessary in all of this, first on the part of the counselor and then, as the dialogue moves along, on the part of the student. So it is at the Institutes as teachers learn to counsel. Although we try as a faculty to express ourselves as precisely as we can, we also depend on metaphor, symbol, inference, and paradox, just as in the counseling dialogue, and we often let questions hang in the air, unanswered, to be pondered by the participants who thereby learn to tolerate the disconnectedness of behavior. The process of the Institute thus once again reflects the process of the counseling dialogue.

Anxiety, ambivalence—perhaps even hypocrisy—may be unavoidable feelings in teachers who are learning to be counselors. Indeed, these feelings occur even in the most committed professionals from time to time. Under these circumstances the counselor is tempted to try to take control as a way of stilling inner anxiety. In this process of trying to gain control, the counselor may become quite impatient as the student goes over the same material again and again.

A few years ago a play called "A Far Country" dramatized a famous case of Freud. It involved a patient who had been mysteriously ill for some time; no one had been able to discover the cause of her illness or find a cure for it. The action of the play concerns Freud's attempts to do just that. In each act, he asks the patient to discuss particular events which, he senses, hold the key to understanding and perhaps to curing her illness. In the course of the play he asks her to review those events repeatedly. She does so with increasing impatience and irritability and to Freud's escalating tension and excitement. Finally, he again asks her the all-too-familiar questions. In a sudden burst of breathless sobs, she tells him more—more than even she was aware she knew—and recounts those same circumstances again but in a uniquely different way. In a powerful and moving third act denouement, she finally says enough to clarify for herself as well as for Freud how and why she became ill, and thus makes it possible to resolve her conflicts and to recover.

Repetitions are not only an essential part of counseling work, they are an unavoidable part of it. Good counseling, indeed, is characterized by repetitions. However things may appear to be the same when they are repeated, there are almost always some differences in meaning when they are presented, and possibly heard, a little differently by both the counselor and the student. Such differences can be liberating for the student and enlightening for the counselor. So the process of the Institutes is characterized by repetitions: similar ideas expressed by different lecturers, various aspects of the same concepts, common themes underscored by all the small group leaders. As the week moves along, ideas that are repeated often have a different ring, modeling in the participant's experience and thus in another way, a counseling dialogue.

Teachers come to the Institutes looking for understanding of what they do as counselors and for answers—particularly for answers. In the Institute, as in counseling, such answers as there are emerge first from the student, then from the dialogue between teacher and student, and lastly—if at all—from the teacher. Over the seven days, the participants learn that *how* we say what we say can also be understood as *what* we say. At first this seems a paradox—substance as process, and process as substance. All of this and more is embedded in the counseling dialogue and reflected in the Institute dialogue. The central business of that dialogue is an attempt, sometimes a quiet struggle and sometimes a noisy one, to hear everything and then to clarify it. This approach makes it possible for the student to liberate his or her feelings, while at the same time controlling his or her behavior. This has very little to do with consistency, which is one of the things that makes counseling so fascinating. It is also one of the things that makes us all work so hard as counselors. Every situation and every person we work with is different; answers are not clear and well defined or readily accessible. Helping teachers to accept that fact is one of the goals of the Institute.

This discussion leads us to the matter of what individual teachers hope to achieve in the counseling process. The goal in the Institute process is to help each teacher define that goal and to scale down expectations about outcome to something modest and thus realistic to achieve. The faculty of the Institute try to support participants as they work at the definition of their expectations, but like most good counselors, the faculty, too, are confined by the reality of their own limitations. They do not aspire to teach teachers to save the world, or even to rescue all of the emotionally downtrodden who come their way. Nor is there any attempt to turn teachers into professional psychotherapists. Our goal is to provide conditions that will enable teachers to grow a little, professionally and personally, to feel a little more confident and comfortable in their work, and to convey that limited kind of expectation to the troubled students who may come to them. This capability should help teachers reduce their unease when listening to someone whose pain is oozing from a well-spring they know little or nothing about and/or have trouble relating to. It should also help limit the discomfort that everyone feels with people whose trouble comes from obvious causes but who cannot understand what those causes are and therefore cannot ease their pain by means perfectly obvious to the counselor but perhaps inappropriate for the student.

It may well be useful at this juncture to address the ways the Institute is structured, and why. The small group meetings are the central experience of the program. Around them we wrap some lectures, some demonstrations of counseling, and various kinds of discussions.

There are many informal discussions. The talk around the dining table is especially productive, being richly laden with criss-crossing veins of information and experience in which everyone shares. The lectures are primarily a way of focusing attention on particular counseling issues, on the process of listening, and on the counseling dialogue.

The structure of the Institute promotes dialogue in which particular emphasis is given to certain key words. Among these words are: feelings, empathy, ambivalence, relationship, ambiguity, anxiety, ventilation, repetition, and above all, *listening* and *clarification*. These words, and the feelings which they identify, occur commonly in the interactions at the Institutes and in the counseling dialogues in which teachers participate at the Institutes and in their work with their students in their schools.

The counselor in the teacher in the person engages the counselee in the student in the person in a reciprocal dialogue, both taking certain risks in doing so. In this dialogue, this relationship, and these encounters, the feelings of both are involved, but the primary goal is to tap into the feelings of the person in the student in the counselee. Role plays are a particularly effective way of demonstrating this goal.

Some role plays are done by the faculty, some by participants, some by both together. It is helpful to know—and it becomes apparent in the course of the week—that the role any of us plays, regardless of the problem or scenario, is ourselves. Playing that role requires us to take the risk of putting something of ourselves on the line and thereby to see more clearly the counselor in the teacher in the person. In doing so, we come to understand ourselves better and become more effective in our role of counseling students. The experience of participating in role playing brings clarity to a number of issues and helps teachers discover themselves in the teacher.

There was a time when the differences between teacher and student in how they thought and lived and felt were substantial. Changes in our current culture have lessened these differences, especially for younger teachers. Their value sets and particularly their life-styles seem to have more commonalities with students than differences. Indeed, these commonalities are quite evident in the process of modeling by teachers and identification of students with them. In many cases there is more of a sharing by peers or, if not peers, friends, as a process of growth. Such relationships are rather different from the classical model of authority figure and subordinate, and it means that the mutuality between counselor and counselee—so important to the counseling dialogue—can be enhanced. This enhancement is reflected in the relationships at the Institute between faculty and participants, the faculty being by and large from an older generation and with years of professional training, yet sharing with the participating teachers, a majority of them young, a great deal in common values and interests. The mutuality that develops over the seven days grows in part out of these similarities.

On the other hand, it is necessary that both teacher and student appreciate that the teacher's role in the counseling relationship is not and cannot be equal to that of the student's. Preserving the real differences in wisdom and experience between teachers and students is at least as healthy for teachers as it is for their students. We try to impress upon the participants the importance of differentiating the adult/teacher role from the student's role and of acting accordingly. In like manner, we as faculty try to be open and accepting in our roles as leaders and "experts," willing to be directive in the small group discussions if need be, even to giving advice at times when that seems useful, and to share our clinical knowledge. To that extent, the process of the Institute illustrates the relationship between the teacher as counselor and the student.

Given the capacities of Institute participants as persons and as teachers and what we hope is a conducive opportunity to learn, participants usually accomplish more than they thought possible. In moving toward that end, they need to appreciate the affective issues as well as the cognitive ones. As the reader has seen, in our goals we emphasize both cognitive and affective matters, but for many teachers a blossoming of affective realization is not their usual experience at an educational institute. How any one teacher comes to grips with the affective side of the experience is an individual matter, but the process is likely to reflect feelings which all of us experience at various times in counseling relationships. Sometimes warm, sometimes disturbing, such feelings are the unavoidable lot of counselors. The personal response of participants to the work at the Institute can be a bit unsettling temporarily, but it can also be gratifying if the teacher can understand what those feelings mean and where they come from. In like manner, if a teacher can develop some insight, then it may be possible to achieve a reasonable degree of control over—or even mastery of—the painful feelings that inevitably arise in counselors. That is one of the hallmarks of growth in anyone—teacher, counselor, or person—and one of the goals of the Institute is to help teachers move significantly in that direction in their own growth.

All of this can be said in a slightly different way. As the Institute moves along, most participants develop a heightened sense of *self*-consciousness, especially in relation to their colleagues. The feeling is likely to be intensified by being in the close company of seventy or so other people, many of whom feel similarly moved, similarly exposed, similarly stimulated, and similarly vulnerable.

The result can make for a delicious but also painful reaction. Indeed the pleasure may be precisely what makes the experience unnerving. It may even present problems in controlling or suppressing impulses. That is a particularly sensitive situation, since most of us have already struggled so hard with the opposite problem—trying to express our feelings. Most participants talk this out with colleagues or with members of the faculty. In so doing they discover that their usual, well-integrated self reasserts control and that such highs are rather temporary and ephemeral. In other words, they use the situation to provide themselves with a kind of *in vivo* experiment in counseling, a recognition that there is great healing power in appreciating one's own reality.

There is much reference throughout the chapters in this book to the importance of risk-taking. Few other learning situations, except perhaps that involved in the practice of clinical therapy, validate more clearly the old cliche about getting out of something just what you put into it. Indeed, teachers may well get somewhat more out of counseling than they put into it if they are willing to assume certain risks. Whatever the risks may be, under the conditions of the Institute they are likely to exist for the most part, only in the perception of the anxious participants—which is risk enough, of course. But one of the goals of the Institute is to provide a uniquely supportive climate in the form of relationships which make it possible for everyone, faculty and participants alike, to make their risks safe ones indeed. Such a supportive climate makes for growth, and growth is as important to teachers as it is to students. Those participants who are willing to invest themselves in the resources the Institute provides are likely to come to recognize longstanding obstacles to their own growth and in some cases, at least, to find ways to resolve some of them in the working-through process that is so central a part of the Institute experience.

In the course of the Institute many of the participants do develop new insights about themselves. One of our goals is that they leave with the clear idea that these insights need to be continually re-examined—that it is useful to rethink the same old things yet again. A little more clarification can come on old issues for any of us if we build the process of rethinking into our self-discipline. One thing which this Institute experience teaches is the value of becoming engaged in an open-ended process of reassessment of one's self. This process provides personal and professional stretch, which stimulates personal and professional growth. That experience is sometimes painful because it may make us anxious, but it is often pleasureable as well because it can lead to further self-discovery—and self-discovery is an essential asset to all of us who offer ourselves as counselors. If we are going to be able to sustain ourselves in the process of resolution of conflict and growth in our student counselees, we must constantly reassess our own reality, our value sets, and our limitations as well as our capacities.

How to bring a counseling process or dialogue to a humane end is a matter of technical and personal concern. Some end by mutual agreement that the counseling tasks are completed or, at least, that a reasonable stopping place has been reached and that the counselor is therefore no longer useful in the counselee's life. Some are terminated in the course of referring the counselee to another helper. Some conclude abruptly, without notice: The counselee simply does not return for an appointment. Such endings usually mean that the counseling work is not fully completed. Some dialogues end in high or hot dudgeon, and some are terminated just by the exigencies of life. Sometimes more than one attempt must be made to bring things to closure. Ideally, effective counseling relationships move gradually and gracefully to an end that is comfortable for the counselor as well as for the counselee.

How to end significant helping/counseling relationships is one of the basic goals of the Institute program, and it applies to participants and faculty alike. Leaving and loss are rarely easy, but they are realities of life, and the attendant feelings need to be acknowledged and often need to be expressed. That happens at the Institute by talking about the feelings involved and by stressing the continuity between the experiences at the Institute and life at the schools to which the teachers will return. We try to make it possible for participants to leave with a sense of revitalization, a questioning mind, and a recognition that much remains unanswered and is yet to be done. In fact, the Institute experience turns out to be, in certain crucial aspects and in its goals, a slice of life. As such we hope it provides participants with a sense of exhilaration about their potential for touching the lives of their students.

INDEX